ANSWERING THE CALL TO EVANGELISM

Spreading the Good News to Everyone

Jack W. Hayford

with
Gary Curtis
and
Robert W. Anderson, Ray Beeson, Gary Howse,
Bob Marshall, Phil Starr

THOMAS NELSON PUBLISHERS
Nashville ● *Atlanta* ● *London* ● *Vancouver*

DEDICATION

This, the third series of
Spirit-Filled Life Bible Study Guides,
is dedicated to the
memory of
Dr. Roy H. Hicks, Jr.
(1944–1994)
one of God's "men for all seasons,"
faithful in the Word, mighty in the Spirit,
leading multitudes into the love of God
and the worship of His Son, Jesus Christ.

Unto Christ's glory and in Roy's memory,
we will continue to sing:

Praise the Name of Jesus,
Praise the Name of Jesus,
He's my Rock, He's my Fortress,
He's my Deliverer, in Him will I trust.
Praise the Name of Jesus.

Words by Roy Hicks, Jr. ©1976 by Latter Rain Music. All rights administered by
The Sparrow Corporation. All rights reserved. Used by permission.

Answering the Call to Evangelism: Spreading the Good News to Everyone
© 1995 by Jack W. Hayford
Published in Nashville, Tennessee, by Thomas Nelson, Inc.

Unless otherwise indicated, Scripture quotations are from
The New King James Bible, © 1979, 1980, 1982,
Thomas Nelson, Inc., Publishers.

Printed in the United States of America
8 — 01 00 99 98 97

CONTENTS

■■

About the Executive Editor/About the Writers.......... 4

The Keys That Keep on Freeing................................. 5

Lesson 1: The Call to Evangelize...................... 10

Lesson 2: Responsibility to Our Generation....... 26

Lesson 3: How to Reach a Person for Jesus 40

Lesson 4: How to Lead a Person to Jesus 54

Lesson 5: Where Are All the Evangelists?........... 64

Lesson 6: Under the King's Call....................... 77

Lesson 7: Compelled by Compassion 87

Lesson 8: Evangelism According to John........... 99

Lesson 9: Evangelism without Fear................... 111

Lesson 10: Taking the Gospel Everywhere 121

Lesson 11: Supernaturally Equipped................... 133

Lesson 12: Evangelizing in the End Times 144

Answering the Call to Evangelism: Spreading the Good News to Everyone is one of a series of study guides that focus exciting, discovery-geared coverage of Bible book and power themes—all prompting toward dynamic, Holy Spirit-filled living.

About the General Editor

JACK W. HAYFORD, noted pastor, teacher, writer, and composer, is the General Editor of the complete series, working with the publisher in the conceiving and developing of each of the books.

Dr. Hayford is Senior Pastor of The Church On The Way, the First Foursquare Church in Van Nuys, California. He and his wife, Anna, have four married children, all of whom are active in either pastoral ministry or vital church life. As General Editor of the *Spirit-Filled Life Bible,* Pastor Hayford led a four-year project, which has resulted in the availability of one of today's most practical and popular study Bibles. He is author of more than twenty books, including *A Passion for Fullness, The Beauty of Spiritual Language, Rebuilding the Real You,* and *Prayer Is Invading the Impossible.* His musical compositions number over four hundred songs, including the widely sung "Majesty."

About the Writers

GARY CURTIS, the writer of two other *Spirit-Filled Life Bible Study Guides,* is an Associate Pastor at The Church on the Way, where he directs the media outreach known as Living Way Ministries.

ROBERT W. ANDERSON, an Assistant Pastor at The Church on the Way, is an author of several children's books and an accomplished writer, director, and award-winning producer and visual designer of films.

RAY BEESON has authored several books and been engaged in full-time ministry since 1975, especially as a teacher edifying the body of Christ through the subjects of prayer and spiritual warfare.

GARY HOWSE, an Assistant Minister at The Church on the Way, has served as a pastor for over twenty years and is now working toward the M.A. in Pastoral Theology.

BOB MARSHALL, on the staff of The Church on the Way, entered full-time ministry after leading lay ministries for over thirty years, before he retired from a career in the communications industry.

PHIL STARR, the Director of World Ministries and Outreach at The Church on the Way, is an experienced equipper of believers for evangelism, having served also as youth minister and missionary.

THE KEYS
THAT KEEP ON FREEING

Is there anything that holds more mystery or more genuine practicality than a key? The mystery: "What does it fit? What can it turn on? What might it open? What new discovery could be made?" The practicality: Something *will* most certainly open to the possessor! Something *will* absolutely be found to unlock and allow a possibility otherwise obstructed!

- Keys describe the instruments we use to access or ignite.
- Keys describe the concepts that unleash mind-boggling possibilities.
- Keys describe the different structures of musical notes which allow variation and range.

Jesus spoke of keys: "And I will give you the keys of the kingdom of heaven, and whatever you bind on earth will be bound in heaven, and whatever you loose on earth will be loosed in heaven" (Matt. 16:19).

While there is no conclusive list of exactly what keys Jesus was referring to, it is clear that He did confer upon His church—upon *all* who believe—the access to a realm of spiritual partnership with Him in the dominion of His kingdom. Faithful students of the Word of God, moving in the practical grace and biblical wisdom of Holy Spirit-filled living and ministry, have noted some of the primary themes which undergird this order of "spiritual partner-ship" Christ offers. The "keys" are *concepts*—biblical themes that are traceable through the Scriptures and verifiably dynamic when applied with soundly based faith under the lordship of Jesus Christ. The "partnership" is the *essential* feature of this release of divine grace; (1) believers reaching to *receive* Christ's promise of "kingdom keys," (2) while choosing to *believe* in the Holy Spirit's readiness to actuate their unleashing, unlimited power today.

Companioned with the Bible book studies in the *Spirit-Filled Life Study Guide* series, the Kingdom Dynamic studies present a dozen different themes. This study series is an outgrowth of the Kingdom Dynamics themes included throughout the *Spirit-Filled Life Bible,* which provide a treasury of insight developed by some of today's most respected Christian leaders. From that beginning, studious writers have evolved the elaborated studies you'll pursue here.

The central goal of the subjects focused on in this present series of study guides is to relate "power points" of the Holy Spirit-filled life. Assisting you in your discoveries are a number of helpful features. Each study guide has twelve to fourteen lessons, each arranged so you can plumb the depths or skim the surface, depending upon your needs and interests. The study guides contain major lesson features, each marked by a symbol and heading for easy identification.

WORD WEALTH

The WORD WEALTH feature provides important definitions of key terms.

BEHIND THE SCENES

BEHIND THE SCENES supplies information about cultural beliefs and practices, doctrinal disputes, business trades, and the like that illuminate Bible passages and teachings.

AT A GLANCE

The AT A GLANCE feature uses maps and charts to identify places and simplify themes or positions.

 ### KINGDOM EXTRA

Because this study guide focuses on a theme of the Bible, you will find a KINGDOM EXTRA feature that guides you into Bible dictionaries, Bible encyclopedias, and other resources that will enable you to glean more from the Bible's wealth on the topic if you want something extra.

 ### PROBING THE DEPTHS

Another feature, PROBING THE DEPTHS, will explain controversial issues raised by particular lessons and cite Bible passages and other sources to which you can turn to help you come to your own conclusions.

 ### FAITH ALIVE

Finally, each lesson contains a FAITH ALIVE feature. Here the focus is, So what? Given what the Bible says, what does it mean for my life? How can it impact my day-to-day needs, hurts, relationships, concerns, and whatever else is important to me? FAITH ALIVE will help you see and apply the practical relevance of God's literary gift.

As you'll see, these guides supply space for you to answer the study and life-application questions and exercises. You may, however, want to record all your answers, or just the overflow from your study or application, in a separate notebook or journal. This would be especially helpful if you think you'll dig into the KINGDOM EXTRA features. Because the exercises in this feature are optional and can be expanded as far as you want to take them, we have not allowed writing space for them in this study guide. So you may want to have a notebook or journal handy for recording your discoveries while working through to this feature's riches.

The Bible study method used in this series revolves around four basic steps: observation, interpretation, correlation, and application. Observation answers the question, What does the text say? Interpretation deals with, What does the text mean?—not with what it means to you or me, but what it meant to its original readers. Correlation asks, What light do other Scripture passages shed on this text? And application, the goal of Bible study, poses the question, How should my life change in response to the Holy Spirit's teaching of this text?

If you have used a Bible much before, you know that it comes in a variety of translations and paraphrases. Although you can use any of them with profit as you work through the *Spirit-Filled Life Kingdom Dynamics Study Guide* series, when Bible passages or words are cited, you will find they are from the *New King James Version* of the Bible. Using this translation with this series will make your study easier, but it's certainly not necessary.

The only resources you need to complete and apply these study guides are a heart and mind open to the Holy Spirit, a prayerful attitude, and a pencil and a Bible. Of course, you may draw upon other sources, such as commentaries, dictionaries, encyclopedias, atlases, and concordances, and you'll even find some optional exercises that will guide you into these sources. But these are extras, not necessities. These study guides are comprehensive enough to give you all you need to gain a good, basic understanding of the Bible book being covered and how you can apply its themes and counsel to your life.

A word of warning, though. By itself, Bible study will not transform your life. It will not give you power, peace, joy, comfort, hope, and a number of other gifts God longs for you to unwrap and enjoy. Through Bible study, you will grow in your understanding of the Lord, His kingdom and your place in it, and those things are essential. But you need more. You need to rely on the Holy Spirit to guide your study and your application of the Bible's truths. He, Jesus promised, was sent to teach us "all things" (John 14:26; cf. 1 Cor. 2:13). So as you use this series to guide you through Scripture, bathe your study time in prayer, asking the Spirit of God to illuminate the text, enlighten your mind, humble your will, and comfort your heart. He will never let you down.

My prayer and goal for you is that as you unlock and begin to explore God's Book for living His way, the Holy Spirit will fill every fiber of your being to the joy and power God longs to give all His children. So read on. Be diligent. Stay open and submissive to Him. You will not be disappointed. He promises you!

Lesson 1 / The Call to Evangelize

When my wife and I moved back to Los Angeles, after living for ten years in the Midwest, we were unprepared for the cultural and demographic changes which had taken place in Southern California during the decade we had been gone. The San Fernando Valley had become home to thousands of foreign immigrants and illegal aliens. What we had known as white suburban neighborhoods were now teeming with thousands of people from other lands, many of whom spoke little or no English.

I remember one Sunday a few weeks after our arrival. After church we wanted to find somewhere to eat lunch. Driving around on some unfamiliar streets, we saw a large building which looked like an oriental pagoda. I was impressed with its design and decor and I thought it might be a lovely Chinese restaurant. When I headed for the parking lot, I was surprised to find that it was a Buddhist Temple—in the middle of the San Fernando Valley!

I always sought to practice and support various forms of evangelism, but my evangelical worldview had always thought of "missions" as primarily raising money to send other Christians to evangelize in foreign countries. I had gone on missions trips to Mexico, but now the mission field had come to me. Here was a large Buddhist Temple less than three miles from two of the largest evangelical churches in America! Suddenly my worldview had to be enlarged to include reaching the people around the corner as well as those overseas.

WORD WEALTH

Love, *agapao* (ag-ah-*pah*-oh); *Strong's #25.* Unconditional love, love by choice and by an act of the will. The word denotes unconquerable benevolence and undefeatable goodwill. *Agapao* will never seek anything but the highest good for fellow mankind. *Agapao* (the verb) and *agapao* (the noun) are the words for God's unconditional love. It does not need a chemistry, an affinity, or a feeling. *Agapao* is a word that exclusively belongs to the Christian community. It is a love virtually unknown to writers outside the New Testament.[1]

So here I am, immersed in a melting pot of ethnic groups and seeking to enlarge my understanding of evangelism. I now see it not just as a call to "reach, win, and teach" people like myself. It is a call that reaches to everyone who has been made in God's image. "Red and yellow, black and white. They are precious in his sight." "For God did not send His Son into the world to condemn the world, but that the world through Him might be saved. He who believes in Him is not condemned; but he who does not believe is condemned already, because he has not believed in the name of the only begotten Son of God" (John 3:17, 18).

WORD WEALTH

Believe, *pisteuo* (pist-*yoo*-oh); *Strong's #4100.* The verb form of *pistis,* "faith." It means to trust in, have faith in, be fully convinced of, acknowledge, rely on. *Pisteuo* is more than credence in church doctrines or articles of faith. It expresses reliance upon and a personal trust that produces obedience. It includes submission and a positive confession of the lordship of Jesus.[2]

The beginning chapters of Genesis reveal that people are a special creation of God and not an advanced stage in a godless evolutionary process. The Bible speaks about our state, status, and station as the delegated authority over the earth and its created order.

How was our "state" revealed in Genesis 1:24–27?

WE WERE MADE IN THE IMAGE OF GOD AND GIVEN ABILITY TO HAVE DOMINION OVER EARTH

What aspects of God's character and personality do you think He chose to reproduce in Adam and Eve when He made them (male and female) "in Our image" ?

SOUL & SPIRIT

What do you think is implied in the command to fill and subdue the earth? (Gen. 1:28)

- BE A GOOD STEWARD W/ WHAT GOD GAVE
- EXPAND THE GARDEN TO THE WHOLE WORLD

Over what was Adam to exercise dominion? (Gen. 1:26–28)

EVERYTHING LIVING ON EARTH

Our status is seen in the special fellowship that the primary human family enjoyed with the Creator, who walked among them "in the garden in the cool of the day" (Gen. 3:8). What does Psalm 8:3–8 say about our status with God?

WE ARE SLIGHTLY LOWER THAN GOD

How did Satan become the "god of this world" and "of this age"? (See John 12:31; 2 Cor. 4:4.)

MAN GAVE IT TO HIM AFTER SINING

How did that affect our "station" as the caretakers of creation?

WE GAVE UP THE RIGHT

KINGDOM EXTRA

In creating man, the Sovereign of the universe makes a choice to delegate to man "dominion . . . on the earth" (Gen. 1:28). Man's power and authority for exercising this rule originate in God's intent to make man in His own image and likeness. Man's ability to sustain his role as delegated ruler of Earth will rest in his continued obedience to God's rule as King of all. His power to reign in life will extend only as far as his faithfulness to obey God's law.[3]

FALLEN MAN

God gave man the capacity of having fellowship with Him at a level unknown among the rest of earth's creatures. But man rejected his God and the place He had given him, and in that choice his state was marred, his status was forfeited, and his station was surrendered.

The means by which sin entered the human race is detailed in Genesis 3, where we are introduced to the subtlety of a cunning serpent.

How do we know this serpent is Satan? (See Revelation 12:9; 20:2)

THE BIBLE SAYS THIS SERPANT WILL BE CAST DOWN

How did this cunning creature create doubt concerning the Word of God? (See Gen. 3:1–5)

- *HE WAS CUNNING*
- *PUT A QUESTION IN THEIR MINDS*
- *TWISTED SCRIPTURE*
- *COMPROMISED / JUSTIFIED*

COVETING

Compare Genesis 3:6 with 1 John 2:15–17 and note how this is a typical pattern of temptation.

— COVETING

AT A GLANCE

TEMPTATION: THE TWO ADAMS CONTRASTED (LUKE 4:1, 2)[4]		
Both Adam and Christ faced three aspects of temptation. Adam yielded, bringing upon humankind sin and death. Christ resisted, resulting in justification and life.		
1 John 2:16	Genesis 3:6 First Adam	Luke 4:1–13 Second Adam—Christ
the lust of the flesh"	"the tree was good for food"	"command this stone to become bread"
"the lust of the eyes"	"it was pleasant to the eyes"	"the devil... showed Him all the kingdoms"
"the pride of life"	"a tree desirable to make one wise"	"throw Yourself down from here"

Rather than debate with the devil, what do New Testament writers stress that we should do? (See 1 Peter 5:8, 9 and James 4:7)

BE AWARE OF THE DEVIL & HIS WAYS

Who was the original sinner? (Gen. 3:6)

DEVIL

Eve disobeyed the Lord's command and ate the fruit first. But Scripture says she was "deceived" (2 Cor. 11:3; 1 Tim. 2:14). Apparently Adam ate knowingly and, as the "federal head" of the human race, initiated the sin principle which Paul presented in Romans 5:12–21. This important precept is summarized in verse 18: "As through one man's offense judgment came to all men, resulting in condemnation, even so through one Man's righteous act the free gift came to all men, resulting in justification of life."

How did original guilt manifest itself with Adam and Eve? (Gen. 3:8)

NAKEDNESS y THEY HID.

In Genesis 3:14–19 a fivefold judgment is pronounced. Identify sin's consequences for those originally involved:

Man - *GROUND CURSED / WORK HARD FOR FOOD / TURN TO DUST*

Woman - *GREAT SORROW / PAINFUL BIRTHS / HUSBANDS WILL BE RULER*

Nature - *THE GROUND IS CURSED*

The Serpent - *CURSED MORE THAN ANIMALS / ON THE BELLY*

The Serpent - *ENMITY BETWEEN SEEDS / HEAD WILL BE BRUISED*

At the same time, a fourfold grace of God is seen in:

- God's seeking out Adam (3:9)
- God's giving them a glimpse of the gospel by promising them a savior (3:15)
- God's clothing them with tunics of animal skin (3:21)
- God's removing them from the Garden of Eden. This removal is gracious because it prevented their eating of the tree of life and thus living forever as sinners separated from God. (Gen. 3:22–24).

FAITH ALIVE

The impact of the "fall" of our original parents has extended to every one of us. Some try to ignore it; others excuse it. But God loves us too much to leave us as we are. He wants us to confess our sins so we can be cleansed (1 John 1:9). When we harbor sin in our lives, we hinder God's plans and purposes for us.

How and why does sinful behavior cause you to seek to avoid contact with God? *GOD IS HOLY AND CAN NOT BE IN THE SAME PLACE WITH SIN, SIN CAUSES A SEPERATION W/ GOD*

How have you been affected by the long-range consequences of sin because of original sin? (See Gen. 3:16, 17–19)

WE ARE SEPERATED FROM GOD BUT WHEN WE ACCEPT JESUS AS OUR SAVIOR WE ARE RE-JOINED WITH HIM

At this point the tree of life disappears from the pages of the Bible until it reappears once again at the end of Scripture during the millennial and eternal ages (Rev. 22:1, 2), where we are finally allowed to eat of its fruit.

 KINGDOM EXTRA

Through disobedience to the terms of his rule, man "falls," thus experiencing the loss of his "dominion" (Gen. 3:22, 23). Everything of his delegated realm (Earth) comes under a curse as his relationship with God, the fountainhead of his power to rule, is severed (vv. 17, 18). Thus, man loses the "life" power essential to ruling in God's kingdom (vv. 19, 22). Beyond the tragedy of man's loss, two other facts unfold. First, through his disobedience to God and submission to the Serpent's suggestions, man's rule has been forfeited to the Serpent. Revelation 12:9 verifies that the spirit employing the snake's form was Satan himself. The domain originally delegated to man now falls to Satan, who becomes administrator of this now-cursed realm. The Serpent's "seed" and "head" indicate a continual line (seed) of evil offspring extending Satan's rule (head) (v. 15). However, a second fact offers hope. Amid the tragedy of this sequence of events, God begins to move redemptively, and a plan for recovering man's lost estate is promised (v. 15) and set in motion with the first sacrifice (v. 21).[5]

"Fallen Man" is more than a theological premise. It is a state of being with eternal consequences. Every day, millions of people who have never heard the Gospel of Jesus are going to their graves. How accountable are we for not having reached them and how accountable are they before God, as Judge, having never heard? Will they go to heaven or hell? *Hell*

Why does God say he will require of us the blood of wicked men? (Ezek. 3:17–19) *God gives a mandate to spread the words of God. When we do not, the blood is on our hands*

What were the responsibilities of the watchman on the walls of ancient Israel? How does Ezekiel 33:1–6 apply to our responsibilities to the lost?

To give warning

Why do people choose to "suppress the truth" they intuitively know about God? (Romans 1:18–20)

THEY HIDE IT WITH UNRIGHTEOUSNESS

Scripture indicates that people are judged according to the revelation of God they know. How will the standard of judgment be different for Jews and Gentiles? (Romans 2:11–16)

ALL MEN ARE JUDGE EQUAL BUT SALVATION IS FOR THE JEW FIRST THEN THE GENTILE.

📖 BEHIND THE SCENES

A recent survey of American adults found that few people could explain the meaning of commonly used religious terms such as the Great Commission (9%), John 3:16 (35%), evangelical (18%), or the gospel (37%). Among adults who describe themselves as "born again" Christians, fewer than expected could correctly explain the four terms: the Great Commission (25%), John 3:16 (50%), evangelical (43%), and the gospel (84%).[6]

Why is everyone considered guilty before God? (Rom. 3:19–23)

WE ARE GUILTY. THE LAW SHOWS US WE ARE SINNERS

Why does Paul indicate the gospel needs to be proclaimed rather than intuitively known? (Rom. 10:11–18)

PEOPLE NEED TO REALIZE AND UNDERSTAND WHAT JESUS HAS DONE. PEOPLE KNOW THERE IS TRUTH, BUT NEED TO BE REVEALED THE TRUTH.

KINGDOM EXTRA

World evangelism requires that we see all people as God sees them—as sinners: 1) by nature (Rom. 3:10); 2) by choice (Rom. 3:23); 3) by practice (Rom. 6:23). Casual attitudes and blinded minds have lured some believers in Christ to overlook the desperate state of the lost: "The wages of sin *is* death" (6:23). Universalism or ultimate reconciliation are terms describing the erroneous belief of some that eventually even the eternally lost will be granted a reprieve from eternal judgment. But Paul said, "We judge thus; that if One died for all, then all died" (2 Cor. 5:14). Because he saw the lost as God sees them, he said God's love "constrained" him to world evangelism. The nations—all people— need the gospel desperately and are lost without it. A clear-eyed look into the Word of God will help us capture and retain the conviction that humankind needs the gospel.[7]

The Father's Plan

History is really "HIS-Story." From the beginning of creation Father God has sought to establish a people over whom He could rule as King. When Adam rebelled against the will of the Authority over him, God made a promise to him that from the seed of woman would come One who would bruise the head of the serpent (Gen. 3:15). This future Seed would establish the Father's kingdom rule on the earth by redeeming us and removing Satan as the "god of this world."

 KINGDOM EXTRA

This verse [Gen. 3:15] contains the first proclamation of the gospel. All of the richness, mercy, sorrow, and glory of God's redeeming work with man is here in miniature. God promised to bring a Redeemer from the Seed of the woman; He was to be completely human, yet divinely begotten. "That serpent of old, called the Devil," would war with the Seed (see Rev. 12) and would smite Him. But even as the Serpent struck at His heel, His foot would descend, crushing the Serpent's head. In Christ's life and death this scripture was fulfilled. Divinely begotten, yet fully human, Jesus, by His death and resurrection, has defeated Satan and made a public spectacle of the powers of hell (Col. 2:15). This first messianic promise is one of the most succinct statements of the gospel to be found anywhere.[8]

Even though they were under the sentence of death, Adam named his wife Eve because she was to be the mother of all living (Gen. 3:20). Eve evidently believed her first son, Cain, was the promised Seed, for she said, "I have acquired a man from the Lord" (Gen. 4:1). When Cain killed his brother Abel, God raised up Seth, whose descendants rebelled against God as well.

Finally, God called Abram, a man of faith from a pagan nation, to start a new nation and become the one through whom He would fulfill His covenant promise to Adam. He did this by making yet another covenant agreement with Abraham and his "seed."

The Abrahamic Covenant (Gen. 12:1–3) can be considered in three sections: 1) personal promises; 2) promises to his seed; 3) promises to all nations. It is given in Genesis 12, and unfolded and enlarged in Genesis 15 and 17.

What were the four specific personal promises made in Gen. 12:2?

1. I WILL MAKE YOU A GREAT NATION

2. I WILL BLESS YOU

3. MAKE YOUR NAME GREAT

4. YOU SHALL BE A BLESSING

KINGDOM EXTRA

In Genesis 12:1–3 God promises to make Abraham great; and God did bless Abraham in many ways, including material blessings. See Genesis 13:1 and 2, where we see how Abraham was made very rich. See also Genesis 24:35, where Abraham's servant reports that "the Lord has blessed my master greatly," and then enumerates the material blessings that God had given to

Abraham. The dynamic of this historic fact becomes pertinent to every believer today.

In Galatians 3:13 and 14, God promises to give all believers the blessings of Abraham, telling us that Jesus became a curse for us so that we might receive "the blessings of Abraham." This begins, of course, with our being born again, or becoming new creatures in Christ Jesus. But "the blessings of Abraham" involve other things as well. The Lord wants us to prosper—spiritually, emotionally, physically, and materially. The blessings are ours by His promise, and we need make no apology for the fact that prosperity is included.[9]

What additional personal promises to Abram can you find in the following verses: Genesis 15:5, 7, 15, 18; 17:4-6?

- MANY DESCENDENTS LIKE THE STARS
- BROUGHT OUT OF UR
- PEACE / OLD AGE

The third section of blessing is known as the "universal promises" because it includes all the families of the earth. Believers of all the ages are saved through the work of Jesus Christ on the Cross. He is the messianic Seed through whom Jew and Gentile are joined.

WORD WEALTH

Families, *Mishpachah* (meesh-pah-*chah*); *Strong's* #4940. A family of people, a type, class, or kind of people or things; a species of animals, a group of related individuals (a tribe), or a group of related things (a category). The main concept of *mishpachah* is that people, animals, or things that share a kinship or similarity of kind form a family, clan, or species. Thus its scope can be as narrow as an immediate family, or as broad as a whole nation (Gen. 10:31, 32; Amos 3:2). Genesis 12:1–3 indicates that God separated Abraham from his idolatrous family in order to make him and his descendants the messianic nation, which would bring salvation to *all* Earth's families.[10]

The Davidic Covenant came about after the people had rejected the theocracy God had intended for Israel. The people had first chosen Saul, and then later accepted David, whom God had chosen (1 Sam. 16:1). God's covenant with David (2 Sam.

7:8–16) indicated a kingdom, or sphere of rule, which would last forever. (Notice, the promise was not that the throne would be occupied forever, but that authority of the kingdom would rule forever.)

Both Mary and Joseph were descendants of David, as detailed in the genealogies of Jesus given in the gospels of Matthew and Luke. Matthew traces the lineage from Abraham to Jesus, while Luke looks back from Jesus to Adam.

 AT A GLANCE

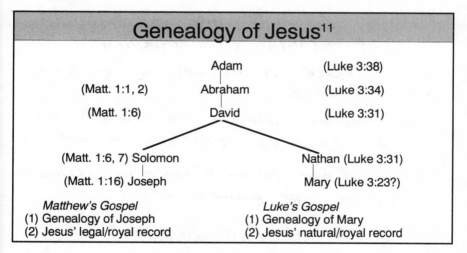

Genealogy of Jesus[11]

	Adam	(Luke 3:38)
(Matt. 1:1, 2)	Abraham	(Luke 3:34)
(Matt. 1:6)	David	(Luke 3:31)
(Matt. 1:6, 7) Solomon		Nathan (Luke 3:31)
(Matt. 1:16) Joseph		Mary (Luke 3:23?)

Matthew's Gospel
(1) Genealogy of Joseph
(2) Jesus' legal/royal record

Luke's Gospel
(1) Genealogy of Mary
(2) Jesus' natural/royal record

Israel was the key instrument the Father chose to use to bring about His master plan to redeem fallen man. For out of Israel (the descendants of Adam, Abraham, and David) would come the Messiah, the Savior-King.

How did the message to Mary by the angel Gabriel fulfill God's promises in the Davidic Covenant? (Luke 1:31–33)

JESUS IS GREAT / SON OF THE HIGHEST / IN THE LINE OF DAVID.

How did Joseph's angelic dream link Mary's pregnancy with the "Seed of the woman" of Genesis 3:15?

MARY WAS A VIRGIN / DID NOT KNOW A MAN

How do each of the following Scriptures reveal the gospel's global purpose?

Genesis 18:18 *A GREAT NATION OF BLESSING*

19:5, 6 *WE ARE TO GO OUT*

22:18 *THE NATIONS WILL BE BLESSED BECAUSE OF ABRAHAM*

26:4 *MULTIPLY & BLESS*

Ps. 72:17–19 *— GOD IS FOREVER & ALL CREATION WILL RECOGNIZE*

Matt. 1:1 *— THERE IS ORDER & A SPECIFIC PURPOSE*

Acts 3:25 *— THROUGH ABRAHAM WE HAVE JESUS WHO BLESSED ALL CREATION FOREVER*

Gal. 3:8–9 *— WE ARE BLESSED THROUGH ABRAHAM HE IS THE FATHER OF FAITH*

The Final Command

Speaking to His disciples after His resurrection, Jesus Christ issued His final command: "You shall be witnesses to Me in Jerusalem, and in all Judea and Samaria, and to the end of the earth" (Acts 1:8). This final call to evangelize was an affirmation of the Great Commission He had given them earlier. To accomplish this task would take the involvement of all the redeemed throughout all of the church age.

PROBING THE DEPTHS

The following five scriptures contain the most succinct references to world evangelization. As you study each passage, note 1) what they have in common, 2) what each scripture adds exclusively to the task's definition and character, and 3) upon what authority Jesus based His command.

Matt. 28:18–20 *WE HAVE AUTHORITY THROUGH JESUS WE ARE MANDATED TO GO OUT*

Mark 16:15–16 (15–20) *WE CAN DO SIGNS & WONDERS IN THE NAME OF JESUS*

Luke 24:46–48 (44–49) *THE NAME OF JESUS PREACH REPENTANCE*

John 20:21–23 ▪ *JESUS IS WITH US, WE HAVE AUTHORITY*

Acts 1:8 (4–8) ▪ *WITNESESS OF JESUS PREACHING IN THE WORLD*

Two thousand years of worldwide evangelism have passed since Christ commissioned His followers to go and proclaim the gospel of the Kingdom. Today, one third of the earth's population declare themselves to be Christians. Whole countries—and even continents—are being loosed from pagan domination. The "Gospel of the Kingdom" is being proclaimed by every means known in every part of the world.

KINGDOM EXTRA

Psalm 2 is a great messianic psalm which discloses the heart of God toward His own Son. "Ask of Me . . . I will give You the nations *for* Your inheritance." This conversation introduces an amazing declaration, that all the nations of the world are intended to come under the aegis of His Son's rule. However, the qualifier is, "Ask." In John 17, through His High Priestly Prayer, Jesus does exactly this (John 17:1–28). However, His request involves our response. We must unite (John 17:21) and we must receive the authority "manifest" in God's name and glory, which Jesus, as the Interceding Messiah of Psalm 2, has conferred upon us—His church. In this name we pray, and by this glory we triumph—receiving the inheritance of nations as God has promised.[12]

In Revelation 7:9–17 we are introduced to "a great multitude which no one could number, of all nations, tribes, peoples, and tongues." Many scholars feel these are "all the redeemed out of all people groups throughout all of history."[13] The supreme task of the church has progressed slowly, but now there is a forceful surge of determination that this task could be accomplished in this generation!

Paul proclaimed in Romans 16:20 the ultimate triumph of Christ and His church over all evil: "And the God of peace will crush Satan under your feet shortly." As we step out in faith to evangelize the lost, whether around the corner or around the world, we are partnering in Satan's ultimate defeat. And, as "the seed of Abraham" (Gal. 3:29), we can take delight in extending God's blessings to the world!

1. *Spirit-Filled Life Bible,* (Nashville: Thomas Nelson Publishers, 1991), 1578, "Word Wealth: John 3:16, loved." The *Strong's* number for Greek words appears in italics, but in regular type for Hebrew words.

2. Ibid., 1704, "Word Wealth: Rom. 10:9, believe."

3. Ibid., 6, "Kingdom Dynamics: Gen. 1:26–28; 2:16, 17, Man's Delegated Dominion."

4. Ibid., 1515, "Temptation: The Two Adams Contrasted (Luke 4:1, 2)."

5. Ibid., 10–11, "Kingdom Dynamics: Gen. 3:16–24, Impact of the Fall."

6. *National & International Religion Report,* March 21, 1994, 1.

7. *Spirit-Filled Life Bible,* 1692, "Kingdom Dynamics: Rom. 3:23, Christ—The Absolute Need of Every Man."

8. Ibid., 9, "Kingdom Dynamics: Gen. 3:15, The Gospel's First Proclamation."

9. Ibid., 22, "Kingdom Dynamics: Gen. 12:1–3, God's Heart to Prosper His people."

10. Ibid., 22, "Word Wealth: Gen. 12:3, families."

11. *Nelson's Complete Book of Bible Maps and Charts* (Nashville: Thomas Nelson Publishers, 1993), 338, "Genealogy of Jesus."

12. *Spirit-Filled Life Bible,* 754, "Kingdom Dynamics: Ps. 2:8, God's Promise to His Messiah."

13. Ibid., 1971, study note on Rev. 7:9.

Lesson 2/Responsibility to Our Generation

If you will "confess with your mouth the Lord Jesus and believe in your heart that God has raised Him from the dead, you will be saved" (Rom. 10:9). Many have come to that beginning point of salvation, but some who have *believed* have not begun to *follow* him as Lord, nor to know the delight and duty of *discipleship*.

A disciple is a believer who has become an ongoing follower of the Lord Jesus and of His methods and means of disciplemaking. Notice the progression: believer, follower, disciple. Can you locate yourself in one of these three categories?

When you acknowledge where you are, ask for God's help in becoming all that He has in mind for you as a devoted disciple.

 KINGDOM EXTRA

There are just two groups of people in this world: those who have heard the gospel and those who have not. If those who have heard (and believed) refuse to tell those who have not heard, God will render to each according "to his deeds." Sobering! While people often debate about those who have died without hearing the gospel, Psalm 24:11 and 12 reveals the soul-stirring importance of seeking those who are alive and have not heard! We cannot go back to the last generation, nor can we reach the next generation, but we can serve this one. The only generation God expects us to be vitally concerned about is our own![1]

What did the early disciples do to learn and demonstrate the "Master's methods" in disciple-making? They chose the **right goals** (to seek disciples and not just decisions), the **right methods** (plow, plant, and harvest), and the **right lifestyles** (Spirit-gifted lives reaching out to edify and evangelize). For us as modern disciples to show responsible ministry toward our generation we must model the goals, methods, and lifestyles of the early disciples.

RIGHT GOALS

After worship, the Bible shows that two other primary goals of the church are to edify other believers and to evangelize.

> And He Himself gave some to be apostles, some prophets, some evangelists, and some pastors and teachers, for the equipping of the saints for the work of ministry, for the edifying of the body of Christ. (Eph. 4:11–12)

> Now all things are of God, who has reconciled us to Himself through Jesus Christ, and has given us the ministry of reconciliation, that is, that God was in Christ reconciling the world to Himself, not imputing their trespasses to them, and has committed to us the word of reconciliation. Now then, we are ambassadors for Christ, as though God were pleading through us: we implore you on Christ's behalf, be reconciled to God. (2 Cor. 5:18–20)

As we move further on in this study guide, we will see how edification and evangelization rub off on one another.

 PROBING THE DEPTHS

In Luke 13:6–9 Jesus told a parable about a barren fig tree. The immediate application was to the nation of Israel, which had failed to produce spiritual fruit. However, we too can learn a lesson about goals and church programs from this parable.

It seems the fig tree had been planted, nurtured, and expected to produce fruit. Certain church programs, too, may have developed over many years, but close analysis reveals that after much work there is still little or no fruit. In many such cases, Jesus' principle is to "cut it down" (v. 7). It is using up time and resources which could be invested with another program.

Yet the hired help urged the owner of the vineyard to wait, in order to "dig around it and fertilize it" for another year. Presumably he had been doing this all along, and his goal was to keep on doing whatever he had been doing. He was "program centered" rather than "goal centered." The owner of the vineyard, however, was concerned with the fruit, the harvest. He had to make the decision whether to continue the program or to "cut it down" and replace it with something which showed more potential.

In thinking of evangelism to "our generation," what programs in your church are bearing fruit and which ones are just "taking up space"?

THE MAIN FOCUS OF THE CHURCH IS MINISTER TO THE NEEDY

Before you "cut it down," do you need to examine if it has had the proper nurture that it needed to succeed?

EVERYTHING DESERVES CAREFUL EXAMINATION GOOD & BAD.

Are your evangelistic goals measurable and reasonable?

YES, IN THE NAME OF JESUS WE CAN REACH THE COMMUNITY & WORLD

RIGHT METHODS

Plow. Some evangelistic efforts do not succeed because care has not been given to prepare the soil for the precious "seed" of the Word. Plowing breaks up the hard surface and helps expose rocks and obstacles which need to be removed before the seed is planted.

Plowing is hard work. It frequently has to be done early, before the heat of the sun is out for the day. It is not glamorous and doesn't have much to show for itself.

What aspects of evangelism could be likened to plowing?

PROVIDING SERVICES & PROGRAMS FOR THE COMMUNITY, BEFRIENDING NON-BELIEVERS

What aspects of your church's ministry could be considered evangelistic preparation?

FEEDING THE HOMELESS / PRAYER TEAMS / ...

Plant. Jesus told of a "sower [who] went out to sow his seed." The means of planting at that time was to dip one's hand in a sack of seed and then "broadcast" it in a spreading motion. The seed fell wherever it landed and some grew and some did not. (See the Parable of the Sower in Matthew 13, Mark 4, and Luke 8.)

The Bible does not give us modern techniques for planting the gospel seed. Psalm 24:1 says, "The earth is the LORD's, and all its fullness, the world and those who dwell therein." We are free to use whatever modern means will glorify God and not detract from the message of the Cross.

List how many means of communication you can think of which might be useful in "planting the gospel seed."

All types of communication
- spoken voice - internet   - hospital visits
- radio   - books
- tv   - door to door - movies

Why are some methods of planting more useful with certain age groups or certain cultures? *Different people learn / recieve differently*

What means have you seen which detracted from the message or diluted its truth?

When there is too much focus on the program or function & not the people

Harvest. God alone can guarantee a harvest. He alone can cause the seed we've planted to grow and then to ripen. "I planted, Apollos watered, but God gave the increase" (1 Cor. 3:6).

But He does not harvest the crop. He requires laborers to discern which fields are now ripe for harvesting, and then to go and "bear much fruit" (John 15:8).

BEHIND THE SCENES

In Jesus' day there were three "fields": Jews, Gentiles, and Samaritans. Early on, only the Jews were the "field" (see Matt.

10:5, 6). Later, both the Gentiles and the Samaritans ripened and bore much fruit for the Kingdom.

RIGHT LIFESTYLES

For many, the most responsible action we can take toward our generation is what some have called "friendship evangelism." This form of outreach takes us to people who perhaps would not be reached in any other way. It requires a sacrifice on our part, a giving, but isn't that what the gospel is all about?

In our Lord's ministry we find an example of "friendship evangelism" in John 4. Why would the Pharisees be concerned with Jesus' ministry at this point in time? (John 4:1, 2)

THEY WERE THREATENED BECAUSE IS WAS DIFFERENT

Why would Jesus need to go through Samaria? (v. 4)

THE WAS A HEAD TO BE MET AND A POINT TO BE PROVEN

BEHIND THE SCENES

In the time of Jesus, Palestine west of the Jordan River was divided into the three provinces of Galilee, Samaria, and Judea. Because of their intermarriage with foreigners, the people of Samaria were shunned by orthodox Jews. Situated between Galilee and Judea, Samaria was the natural route for traveling between those two provinces. But the pure-blooded Jews had no dealings with the Samaritans (John 4:9). They would travel east, cross the Jordan River, and detour around Samaria.[2]

What time of day did this incident take place, by Jewish reckoning? (John 4:6)

ABOUT THE 6th HOUR

How would that help to explain where the disciples were? (v. 8) *IT WAS TIME TO EAT*

How does the moral condition of the Samaritan woman explain why she might be coming to the well in the heat of the day? (v. 18) *THE OTHER WOMEN DID NOT WANT HER AROUND AND OR SHE DID NOT WANT TO BE AROUND THEM.*

This story reveals several lessons for responsible evangelism to our generation. *JESUS USED WHAT WAS FAMILIAR TO THE WOMEN*

WE MUST CONTACT OTHERS SOCIALLY

Make no mistake. Separation from the things of the world is not optional for the Christian. It is mandatory. "Come out from among them and be separate from them, says the Lord" (2 Cor. 6:17).

From what are we specifically told to abstain?

1 Thess. 5:22 - *EVERY FORM OF EVIL*

1 Pet. 2:11 - *FLESHLY LUSTS*

What is the implied answer to Paul's question on fellowship in Second Corinthians 6:14?

RIGHTEOUSNESS CANNOT FUNCTION W/ SIN

In thinking about our efforts in evangelism, many will come to the painful realization that we have a limited opportunity to witness because we have few non-Christian friends. Certainly, God's intention is that we be insulated from the attitudes and activities of this world, but not isolated from them. However, for some, our commitment to service within the church has cut off our contact and fellowship with those outside the church. Our pool of non-Christian friends has dried up.

Jesus prayed to the Father in John 17:15, "I do not pray that You should take them out of the world, but that You should keep them from the evil one." Our lost friends are the ones who need our friendship and God's forgiveness.

In Luke 5:30–32, why did the Pharisees complain against Jesus' disciples?

THEY WERE EATING WITH SINNERS

Write out Jesus' response to them (vv. 31–32):

- JESUS CAME FOR SINNERS
- A DOC HELPS THE SICK NOT THE WEL

Describe the physical appearance of the woman Jesus met at the well in John 4.

SHE WAS A WOMAN IN NEED

Describe the emotional state of this woman (rejected by five husbands and living with a sixth without the commitment of marriage).

HOPELESS / HURT / UNLOVED / DEAD

What did Jesus offer as a solution to her problem?

HOPE / LIFE / LOVE / FREEDOM

Does His solution have any relevance to the needy people in our world? If so, how does it become operational in our experiences?

THROUGH JESUS WE CAN OFFER
LIFE / LOVE / LIBERTY

WE MUST GO WHERE NON-CHRISTIANS ARE

The Cross must be raised in the marketplace as well as on the steeples of the churches. We cannot hope to get our entire communities into our churches to hear evangelistic sermons (as valid and proven as this method of evangelism is). But we can hope to get our churches (born again believers; devoted disciples) out into every area of our communities.

How did the mob in Thessalonica describe the evangelistic effectiveness of the early disciples? (Acts 17:6)

The disciples did not have evangelistic success by only inviting people to church with them. They did it by reaching out to people in non-Christian settings. Read the following scriptures and identify some of the various places Paul presented the gospel.

Acts 16:11–13 *OUTSIDE THE CITY*

Acts 16:14-15 *GOING TO PEOPLES HOUSE*

Acts 16:16–34 *IN STREETS / PRISON / HOUSE*

Acts 20:20 *PUBLICLY / IN HOMES*

Peter and John said they couldn't restrain their desire to witness for the Lord Jesus: "We cannot but speak the things which we have seen and heard!" (Acts 4:20).

 KINGDOM EXTRA

In the Bible we find four points of "friendship," or "lifestyle," evangelism.

1. *The Holy Spirit will prepare the harvest field for you.*

2. *The Holy Spirit will lead you.* Psalm 37:23 says, "The steps of a good man are ordered of the Lord." And Paul taught that "it is God who works in you both to will and to do for His good pleasure" (Phil. 2:13).

3. *The Holy Spirit will empower and guide you.* An open door is often a spiritual, emotional, physical, or material need which you discern in someone.

4. *The Holy Spirit remains active in lives after your initial contact* (John 4:39–42).

Jesus went to a public gathering place and proceeded to establish an opportunity for presenting truth which transformed an entire town!

ESTABLISH COMMUNICATION BRIDGES

Jesus did not begin by telling the Samaritan woman she was a sinner and He alone could save her. Sometimes we let the pressure to witness build and then explode like a time bomb of scripture verses. He began with something she was obviously interested in and built a bridge for further communication. We have to win the right to be heard.

This is where friendship evangelism excels. We are not concerned just with presenting them with doctrine but in ministering to them as people, people with needs, feelings, and doubts. If they don't like us, it isn't very likely they will be interested in our message.

FAITH ALIVE

Romans 10:13 and 14 says, "For whoever calls upon the name of the Lord shall be saved. How then shall they call on Him in whom they have not believed? And how shall they believe in Him of whom they have not heard? And how shall they hear without a preacher?"

If you would experience the delight of life-style evangelism:

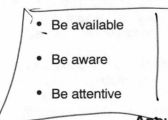

- Be available

- Be aware

- Be attentive

AROUSE CURIOSITY

We can arouse curiosity by what we do. The Samaritan woman was surprised that a Jew would talk to her. She was a woman in a patriarchal culture. He was a holy man, a Rabbi. Furthermore, the "Jews [had] no dealings with the Samaritans" (John 4:9). Yet Jesus befriended her.

As Christians we are to be possessed by a deeper purpose in life. *Our attitudes* toward people are to be loving, considerate, kind, and long-suffering. *Our reactions* to circumstances are most telling when we demonstrate complete trust in the will of God. *Our actions* in the course of our daily duties may be the turning point in our contact with that non-Christian friend. An act of kindness, unselfish love, may be the key to someone's soul. We can draw people to Jesus by living on the outside the changed life that we have on the inside.

We can also arouse curiosity by what we say. The Lord tactfully and lovingly coaxed the Samaritan woman into asking a question. He baited the hook. To be effective "fishers of men" we must first learn to be skillful baiters of hooks.

 FAITH ALIVE

Some have found simple questions to be helpful. Something like:

"Do you ever give much thought to spiritual things?"

"Have you every thought of becoming a Christian?"

"If someone were to ask you, 'What is a real Christian?' what would you tell them?"[3]

Learn to be alert to everyday experiences. Throw out a leading comment, and plan ahead for common remarks in everyday conversation. For example, someone may ask, "Why are you so happy?" Then you can share your spiritual experiences. Or you might respond to their frustrations by saying, "You know, I used to feel that way." Or, "You know, I would feel that way if it were not for. . . ."

Another way to arouse curiosity and draw people into a conversation of spiritual issues is to be alert to current events. Crime, economics, sickness, medical cures, and many other topics all have the potential of attracting spiritual interest.

DON'T GO TOO FAR

Despite the Samaritan woman's obvious interest and curiosity, Jesus didn't give her the whole story at once. The Holy Spirit must prepare the heart. We cannot create interest; only God can. If the person doesn't become interested immediately, we can leave the subject and come back at a later time to pick it up. Don't frighten the person off by coming on too strongly. A bird is scared from its perch by too rapid a movement.

Don't Condemn

Our Lord allowed this woman's sin to condemn her by itself. We are to witness of His love and grace. It is the role of the Holy Spirit to convict of sin and to convince of righteousness. How many have been turned off by self-righteous condemning people? *Matt 4*

Faith Alive

A drunken and profane man sat beside an evangelist on a train and offered him a drink. The wise evangelist responded, "No thank you, but I can see that you are a gracious man."

How would you have handled the situation? "No thank you, I don't drink, I'm a Christian." If this were your response, you have condemned the person. You have implied that you are more holy than he is, when all of us are "sinners saved by grace." You have also confused the gospel. The essence of Christianity is not whether you drink or don't drink. Temperance is a fruit of the spirit, not the root of it.

Win friends and influence them for Christ. Look for opportunities to live graciously in a non-Christian society. Don't let your good be spoken of as evil (Rom. 14:16). Look for opportunities to compliment rather than condemn.

Stick with the Main Issue

Our Lord could have challenged her theology or her patriotism, but he did not allow her to sidetrack Him. He stuck with the main issue: her need for a personal relationship with God the Father (John 4:21).

What side issue did she seek to introduce into the discussion? (John 4:20)

THE PROBLEM BETWEEN JEWS / SAMARITANS

What is more important, where one worships, or the attitude of the heart and mind?

HEART / MIND

 PROBING THE DEPTHS

Within the context of the diverse, larger body of Christ, various viewpoints on doctrine, denominational emphases, and ministry styles bring confusion to the contemporary mission of the church. Because of this broad diversity, the Adversary cleverly and treacherously seeks to entrap us in an arrogant mind-set, which will misdirect the church from its central mission.

Use your commentaries, concordances, and other resources to help you probe the following questions:

How did Jesus discern divine direction? (Matt. 4:8–10)

JESUS RECOGNIZED THE TEMPTATION DECEPTION

How did Jesus alert the disciples to Satanic deception in the end-times? (Matt. 24:4, 5, 11–14)

DECEPTION

How did Paul teach the church at Corinth about ministry misdirection? (2 Cor. 11:12–15)

THERE WERE SOME BEING DECEIVED

How did Paul warn the church of being off course into futility and perverted logic in Romans 1:21 and 22?

DON'T BE DECEIVED

How did Paul guide young believers in First Corinthians 15:33 and 34?

CHECK ALL TEACHING WITH THE WORD OF GOD / SCRIPTURE

BRING PEOPLE TO CONFRONTATION WITH CHRIST

It is not enough to talk *about* Jesus or spiritual things. A listener must make a *personal decision* about Christ. Salvation is a gift. One either accepts it (on His conditions) or rejects it.

Sometimes we are hesitant to be so direct. We may be afraid because we fear it may bring our friendship to an end. Yet we see signs that say, "Friends don't let their friends drive drunk." In a similar sense, "Real friends don't want their friends to miss heaven and end up in hell."

PROBING THE DEPTHS

Proverbs 24:11–12, when presented with evangelistic fervor, points out one of the most awesome obligations for which we are to be accountable:

Deliver those who are drawn toward death, And hold back those stumbling to the slaughter. If you say, "Surely we did not know this," does not He who weighs the hearts consider it? He who keeps your soul, does He not know it? And will He not render to each man according to his deeds?

What is our responsibility? *GIVING OTHERS THE POSSIBILITY*

How does verse 12 fix our accountability?
W/E ARE ACCOUNTABLE FOR OTHERS TO BELIEVE

We can see in these scriptures our responsibility to "rescue the ignorant headed for destruction. God will not accept our excuses."[4]

 ## FAITH ALIVE

Perhaps these three points summarize responsible witnessing:

1. We shouldn't pressure a person to receive Christ. Only the Holy Spirit can bring a person to this commitment.
2. Let a person know in advance that your friendship does not depend upon his or her response to Christ.

3. But *do* invite the person to receive Him personally. "Does this make sense to you, Charlie? Would
you like to receive Christ now?"

REAP THE RESULTS

These principles of evangelism worked for Jesus (John 4:39–
42)! They will work for you too. But like all rules for success, they
will not work unless you do. If you will cultivate the ground and
plant the seed, you can expect to reap the resulting harvest for
Christ. Evangelism is not optional. We are commanded to serve
the Lord by reconciling sinful man with a holy and loving God.
What are we doing about it?

Getting our own lives into alignment with our Lord, His
character and purpose, is vital. Enthroning Jesus as Lord in our
own lives is what finally determines which activities will get the
energy bursts needed for us to reap evangelistic results.

In helping us to prioritize our lives and our lives' activities,
how do you see Jesus' statement, "If any man will be my disciple,
let him deny himself, take up his cross and follow me" (Luke
9:23)?

 FAITH ALIVE

Below, write how you see yourself responding to the above
verse in relation to ministry to our generation in the light of
Proverbs 24:11 and 12.

ACKNOWLEDGE THE RESPONSIBILITYS

AND LOOK FOR OPPORTULITIES

1. *Spirit-Filled Life Bible* (Nashville: Thomas Nelson Publishers, 1991), 915, "Kingdom Dynamics: Prov. 24:11–12, Committed Action to Our Generation."

2. *Nelson's Illustrated Bible Dictionary* (Nashville: Thomas Nelson Publishers, 1986), 941,
"Samaria."

3. C. S. Lovett, *Soul-Winning Made Easy* (Baldwin Park, CA: Personal Christianity), 1959.

4. *Spirit-Filled Life Bible,* 914, study note on Prov. 24:11–12.

Lesson 3/How to Reach a Person for Jesus

One of the most amazing accounts of a person's coming to know Jesus is found in Acts 8:26–38, when the Lord directed Philip to the Ethiopian eunuch. We don't know the man's name, but he was a eunuch of great authority under Candace, queen of Ethiopia, and he had come to Jerusalem to worship.

While the eunuch sat in his chariot reading from the Book of Isaiah, the Holy Spirit spoke to Philip, "Go near and overtake this chariot." As Philip ran to him he heard him reading and said, "Do you understand what you are reading?" The man responded, "How can I, unless someone guides me?" He then invited Philip to come up and sit with him. The place in the Scripture which he read was this:

> He was led as a sheep to the slaughter; and as a lamb before its shearers is silent, so He opened not His mouth. In His humiliation His justice was taken away, and who will declare His generation? For His life is taken from the earth.

The eunuch then said, "I ask you, of whom does the prophet say this, of himself or of some other man?" Philip responded and, beginning at this Scripture, preached Jesus to him.

SCRIPTURE AND SOUL WINNING

Before we consider our role in bringing people to Christ, we must first recognize God's heart in the matter. What does the Scripture say about the eternal condition of all humanity? (John 3:3; Eph. 2:12)

What does the Scripture say about God's desire for all humanity? (John 6:37; 2 Pet. 3:9)

ALL WHO COME TO JESUS WILL BE SAVED

What is our primary responsibility in winning the lost? (Acts 1:8)

BE WITNESSES

In God's plan we are to work with Him for the salvation of souls (1 Cor. 3:9), but who is it that actually causes a person to come to the Lord? (John 6:44)

HOLY SPIRIT

The Scripture makes it clear that *we* can't save anyone—only God can. At the same time God asks for our assistance through witnessing. As we declare what we know and what we have seen, God uses that testimony to bring people to Himself. But our testimony is not to be so much what God has done for us as it is to be a declaration of our understanding of who Jesus is. Remember from our text that Philip began at the Scripture and preached Jesus. How do you think Philip presented Jesus?

List three ways in which we can "preach" Jesus.

1) *TESTIMONY*

2) *SCRIPTURE*

3) ~~*GIVING HOPE*~~ *WITNESS*

BEING WITNESSES

Jesus has called us to be witnesses. By divine commission we are to tell the world about Jesus. What is it that we are actually commissioned to do? (Mark 16:15)

WITNESS

4. What do we really mean by a Christian witness, and with what ability or strength do we carry it out?

LIVE AND SPEAK SO THAT OTHERS MAY KNOW & GROW

Notice that there is a great deal of Christian activity that goes on, presumably to be a witness, but it is motivated by far less than a sensitive understanding of what it actually means to be a witness. There are many people who feel, "I just couldn't witness because I don't have the boldness of other people." Yet the Bible says nothing about being a witness on the grounds of some natural boldness we may have. The majority of us feel a certain degree of timidity. We don't want anyone to feel we are imposing ourselves, especially when it comes to spiritual matters. When the Lord said we will be His witnesses, He was not saying something that would be impractical for any of us. So there must be a way for this to happen for all of us, as opposed to its being something that only a handful of select personality types can do.

WORD WEALTH

Witness, *martus* (*mar*-toos); *Strong's #3144.* Compare "martyr" and "martyrdom." One who testifies to the truth he has experienced, a witness, one who has knowledge of a fact and can give information concerning it. The word in itself does not imply death, but many of the first-century witnesses did give their lives, with the result that the word came to denote a martyr, one who witnesses for Christ by his death.[1]

A witness is evidence in a case, a person who has, presumably, some credibility on the subject because of experience, which shows in their own convictions. A witness is called to be a spokesperson for the issue on trial. To be a witness, then, is to have the character of the Lord working in us so that we are credible to people.

What's on trial in the world today is whether or not Jesus Christ is believable as the Son of God, whether or not He's powerful as the Savior of the world, and whether or not He is genuine in what He brings to a person's life.

HOLY SPIRIT ENABLING

In recognizing that we are called by Jesus to be witnesses, it's important that we see that He will give the power of the Holy Spirit to make it happen. That recognition and a subsequent relying on His help begins the process for effective witnessing. When all elements of strength, ability, boldness, and even desire seem gone, God's mightiness is there to draw on. Never try to extend God's Kingdom without his help and direction.

How and when do we receive Holy Spirit power? (Acts 1:8)

WHEN WE ASK WE WILL RECEIVE

What is a primary reason for the Holy Spirit's power in the life of a believer? (Acts 1:8)

WITNESSING

How much can we do for the Kingdom of God on our own? (John 15:5)

NOTHING

AN EVANGELISTIC FAITH

A living, vital, Holy Spirit-filled Christianity is an evangelistic faith. The Spirit of God, alive in us, causes us to reach out and touch others with the gospel ("the good news"). To evangelize means to spread the gospel. And we are evangelistic when we are committed to evangelism.

To be evangelistic means that we focus on the good news, not on the bad.

The good news is that the grace of God draws men unto Himself (John 12:32). When God is lifted up in the presentation of His love in the person of Jesus Christ, and when the gentleness of Christ is seen in that presentation, people come to know Jesus.

However, there's just enough religiousness in most of us to feel that our job is to convince people that, yes, God is loving and kind, but we are sinful; and if you don't do something about your sin you are going to be lost forever. Somehow we feel our job is to focus only on the bad news.

But notice what Jesus said on the night He was crucified, knowing full well the price it was going to cost Him to provide eternal salvation for all of us. He said, "I'm going to send the Holy Spirit, and when He comes He will convince of sin and of righteousness and of judgment." He says the Holy Spirit will convict.

Let the Holy Spirit convince people of their sinfulness and their need. Our call is not to point the bony figure of self-righteousness and tell people how hellbound they are. The Holy Spirit can well take care of that. We are called to trust the Holy Spirit to draw people when we exalt Jesus.

We are called to spread good news. And the good news isn't that all have sinned and come short of the glory of God. The good news is not that the wages of sin is death. There is nothing good about sin or eternal condemnation. Certainly it is true, and it is not a matter we are to contest. But at the same time it isn't our focus. We are called to reach the world with the healing, powerful, loving, living Jesus, whom we preach. And *that* is good news!

List three ways that we can exalt Jesus (Mic. 6:8; Eph. 5:17–21; Phil. 2:5).

1) LOVE MERCY / TO DO JUSTLY / WALK HUMBLY

2) BE FILLED W/ THE SPIRIT / WORSHIP TOGETHER GIVE THANKS / RESPECT ONE ANOTHER

3) HAVE THE MIND · OF CHRIST

To be evangelistic means that we issue an invitation, not practice coercion.

There is a word bandied around in our society about Christian evangelism. The word frequently crops up in the press and on talk shows: "proselytize," which means to recruit members from one faith or religious tradition to another by offering special inducements or requirements at pressure. Yet this is not what we are seeking to do. Our objectives are not to convert people from one faith to another faith or tradition but to see people saved. Proselytizing is about coercion tectics, and it has nothing to do with changing a heart.

 BEHIND THE SCENES

In the eleventh and twelfth centuries of the Middle Ages, Crusaders went forth in a series of "holy" wars under the banner of the Cross and in the name of Jesus Christ. As they came into countries where there were Muslim and Jewish traditions, they would force people at the pain of death to convert and become "Christians." Understandably many people "converted," though many were also killed. It's a tragic fact of Christian history that it occurred; and even more, that it happened in the name of Jesus.

There's no good news about forcing people into a religious belief. That isn't evangelism. It's proselytism, which involves coercing people from one religious conviction to another. Even then, the new conviction isn't real; it's only an accommodation because the person changed under some threat.

List attitudes and characteristics of a person who witnesses under the influence of the Holy Spirit, according to the following verses:

2 Cor. 10:1   *Humble / Bold*

Gal. 5:22   *Being the fruit of the Spirit*

Phil. 1:16, 17 · *UNSELFIS / LOVING*

Notice a certain characteristic that was not in Jesus and should not be found in us, especially when we witness. See John 3:17 and Romans 8:1. What is it?

NO CONDEMNATION
BUT SALVATION

BEHIND THE SCENES

In the last century or two, "rice bowl" Christians are found in some parts of the Orient. Some missionaries went into certain environments to evangelize, while at the same time offering food resources that the people didn't have. But they could get the food if they would convert to the faith of those who brought the gospel. And so, there became large numbers of "rice bowl Christians." That wasn't evangelism. At best it was a charitable effort to feed people. At worst it was proselytism, an inducement for people to realign their religious identification on the basis of physical hunger.

To be evangelistic means that we depend on the divine power of God, not on human programs.

Because God sometimes seems far away, it's easy to believe that He gave us responsibilities and tasks to accomplish and then left us on our own to do them. This is far from the truth, especially in view of the many scriptures which emphasize that the Holy Spirit is at work among us. Read the following scriptures for understanding the work of the Holy Spirit and record your thoughts about His work. (John 14:16–17; 15:26; Acts 2:8; Rom. 8:26; 1 John 4:4)

List three ways in which divine power is imparted to the believer.

Ps. 119:11; 1 Tim. 2:15

Acts 4:31; Col. 4:2

Acts 2:1; Heb. 10:25

DRAMA LESSONS

Notice the drama of events and the lessons to be learned from them in Acts 8:26–38.

The Place (v. 26): Philip was directed by God to meet a unique need in an odd place.
The Lesson: Be open to unusual leadings from God.

Has God ever directed you to someone in order to share the Gospel? *yes - sometimes I have but there have been times when I have not*

How can we be more open to the Holy Spirit to be used for witnessing?
constantly being open and available for God to speak to us and use us.

 ### AT A GLANCE

The Person (v. 27): The Ethiopian eunuch was searching and open for truth.
The Lesson: Be aware of and sensitive to people who are open to Jesus but still don't know Him.

Who do you see searching for truth? *some friends & family*

In what ways are they searching and open?
- they ask questions
- attracted to the people of God

The Time (v. 29): The Spirit said go.

The Lesson: Be sensitive to the Holy Spirit's prompting.

Philip's Missionary Journeys. Two journeys are recorded in Acts 8:5–13 and 8:26–40.

Do you think Philip heard God audibly?

I BELIEVE HE WAS CERTAIN HE HEARD GOD

Do you understand what it means for God to speak to your heart?

YES

The Cue (v. 30): Philip heard the eunuch reading from Isaiah.

The Lesson: Watch and listen for openings and contexts in which to talk about Jesus.

Can you think of anyone right now who would be open to talking about Jesus?

YES

What have you seen about the person that make you think he or she is open?

ASK QUESTIONS AND ARE OPEN TO LISTEN

The Question (v. 30): Philip asked him about what he was reading.

The Lesson: Appropriate questions usually further a person's interest.

What questions could you ask your person about Jesus?

WHAT DO YOU THINK ABOUT WHAT WE TALKED ABOUT

What could you say to open the subject?

HELLO, HOW ARE YOU

The Presentation (v. 35): Philip preached Jesus.
The Lesson: When a person seems open, boldly preach Jesus.

As you preach Jesus, what is it you are going to say about Him? List several things so that you are prepared.

1) HEED FOR JESUS

2) YOU HAVE PURPOSE

3) JESUS IS THE ANSWER

WORD WEALTH

Preached, *kerusso* (kay-*roos*-oh); *Strong's #2784.* To herald, tell abroad, publish, propagate, publicly proclaim, exhort, call out with a clear voice, communicate, preach. The herald is to give a public announcement of an official message and to issue whatever demands the message entails. The Christian herald is to proclaim the message of salvation through Jesus Christ and issue a summons to repent and receive forgiveness of sins.[3]

To "preach" does not mean to stand in front of an audience and yell Bible verses. It means to speak about good news of Jesus.

The Decision (vv. 36–38): The eunuch believes and is baptized.
The Lesson: Lead people to decisive action when they are ready and willing.

What is the best time to come to know Jesus? (Heb. 3:12–15; 4:7)

WHEN THE PERSON HAS THE DESIRE WHEN THEY HEAR & THE HEART IS SOFT

When someone comes to know Jesus, what happens in heaven? ANGELS REJOICE / THERE IS NEW LIFE

Phil. 4:3   JESUS WRITES THE NAME OF THE LAMBS BOOK OF LIFE

Luke 15:10

Thousands of "Coptic Christians," in Ethiopia and around the world, trace their Christianity back to this eunuch's conversion. An entire nation was affected by God's work through Philip that day.

FAITH ALIVE

Praying for those you want to see come to Jesus is important. The following is a list of things you might want to pray.

Father God, cause _____ (name) to become aware of his or her need of salvation.

Father, lead other Christians also to witness to _____ (name).

Lord, keep the enemy from destroying the seed we are working to plant in _____ (name).

Lord, give me wisdom and understanding as I minister to _____ (name).

Father, help me to show _____ (name) the love of Jesus.

Talk to God occasionally about your concern for those you desire to see come to Jesus. Tell Him exactly what you are thinking and feeling about each situation. Then believe Him to do what you cannot do on your own.

TIMES AND SEASONS FOR EVANGELISM

Notice the seasonal steps involved in leading people to Christ. Each is important in its own way, and all are related to conversion and subsequent growth in Christ.

1. Sowing the seed

List at least three people around you whom you would like to see come to Jesus.

1) FAMILY

2) FRIENDS

3) PEOPLE IN COMMUNITY

What could you do in the near future to plant the seed of the Gospel in them?

1) BE A WITNESS

2) BEFRIEND THEM

3) TALK WITH THEM

2. Watering the seed

List what you could do to keep these persons progressively aware of their need for Jesus.

1) BE A WITNESS

2) TALK WITH THEM

3) OPEN TO ANSWER ANY QUESTIONS

3. Patiently watching for growth and praying

Write down several things you are asking God to do towards growth in the lives of these people.

1) GOD TO PROVIDE MORE OPPORTUNITIES TO SHARE

2) *HOLY SPIRIT TO OPEN EYES*

3) *GOD TO PROVIDE OTHER BELIEVERS IN THEIR LIFE.*

4. Reaping the harvest

Keep a list of relevant scriptures and ideas to use when leading a person to Christ. Make the list below.

1) *ROMANS ROAD*

2) *GOD HAS PURPOSES*

3) *JESUS IS THE ANSWER*

5. Caring for the harvest

List several things you will do for these people after they have become Christians.

1) *PRAY*

2) *BE WITNESS*

3) *TALK WITH*

FAITH ALIVE

Samuel Zwemer, one of the first ministers to take the Gospel to the Muslim world, was about to depart England for Egypt when someone said to him, "How do expect to convert a Muslim to Christianity?" Zwemer replied, "I don't expect to convert any Muslims to Christianity. I expect to win people to the Person of Jesus."

Perhaps you have been the kind of person who believed that force was the only real way to win the lost. Or maybe you have felt the timidity that so many of us do when it comes to witnessing. Yet you would like to be used of the Lord in the harvest.

If that is your desire, you might want to begin by praying the following prayer:

> Father God, I have come to recognize some valuable truths for winning the lost. I admit that I have made some mistakes in the past in my approach to being a soul winner. I want you to use me to touch the lives of people who need Jesus. Use my lips, my hands, my feet, my talents, and the resources you have given me to make this happen. I thank you for hearing my prayer because I know that you want people to come to know Jesus.

1. *Spirit-Filled Life Bible* (Nashville: Thomas Nelson Publishers, 1991), 1960, "Word Wealth: Rev. 1:5 witness."

2. Ibid., 1640.

3. Ibid., 1642, "Word Wealth: Acts 9:20 preached."

Lesson 4/ How to Lead a Person to Jesus

In John 3:1–8 there is the familiar story of the encounter between Jesus and Nicodemus. This has become famous if only because it introduced terminology that has gone from being the deepest meaning of regenerated life to the shallowest.

In our society the term "born again" is not only used as a sometimes derogatory Christian label, but it has been applied to motorcycles, laundry soap, and tennis stars! Nevertheless, "born again" is a biblical term from Jesus' own lips: "Do not marvel that I said to you, 'You must be born again'" (John 3:16).

BEHIND THE SCENES

Nicodemus ("Conqueror of the People") was a Pharisee and member of the Sanhedrin. He was familiar with Jewish law, history, and custom and was easily aware of the prophecies concerning the Messiah. It appears that many of the people of Jesus' day who were interested in a Messiah were concerned about the present Roman oppression and wanted their freedom from it. Whether or not this was a concern of Nicodemus's is difficult to tell, since the Sanhedrins were granted civil authority under Roman rule. But his interest in Jesus was, perhaps, compromised by his concern over his reputation and position. This may be why he came to Jesus by night. It appears, however, that Nicodemus became a believer because he helped prepare the body of Jesus for burial (John 19:39–42).

To be "born again" means to experience a new kind of life in which the human spirit becomes "alive" to God. This is not a second biological birth, of course, but a spiritual one in which we are "born from above." A person is literally introduced into a new realm in which he can realize, experience, and communicate with God. Sometimes we use the term "saved" or "converted" to acknowledge this new birth experience.

To whom must we turn, specifically, to discover this "born again" or salvation experience? (John 14:6; Acts 4:12)

COMING TO CHRIST

Let's look at some of the steps involved in the salvation process. Look up the scriptures and fill in the blanks.

(John 1:12) As many as _RECEIVED_ Him, to them He gave the right to become children of God.

WORD WEALTH

Redeemed, *ga'al* (gah-*ahl*); *Strong's #1350.* Ransom, redeem, repurchase; to set free by avenging or repaying. *Ga'al* refers to the custom of buying back something a person has lost through helplessness, poverty, or violence. Furthermore, the one who does the redeeming is often a close relative who is in a stronger position and buys back the lost property on behalf of his weaker relative. Psalm 72 is universally understood as speaking of the Messiah; v. 14 states "He will redeem [*ga'al*] the life of the needy from oppression and violence." In Isaiah 52:9, God redeems Jerusalem, buying it back from its oppressors on behalf of His people. The biblical view of redemption is extremely wide, for God has pledged to redeem the whole creation, which currently groans in bondage (Rom. 8:20–23).[1]

In Titus 2:14, from what does Paul teach we are redeemed?

SIN   & DEATH

Who or what holds us in captivity? (Rom. 7:23)

SATAN

What is the "currency" God uses to pay for our release from captivity? (Rev. 5:9)

BLOOD

(Acts 3:19) __*REPENT*__ therefore and be converted, that your sins may be blotted out.

✎ WORD WEALTH

Ransom, *lutron* (*loo*-trahn); *Strong's #3083.* From the verb *luo,* "to loose." The word signifies a release from slavery or captivity brought about by the payment of a price. Sin demands an expiation, an atonement, a price paid because of the penalty of death that was upon us. Jesus' gift to us was Himself, a universal ransom (for many) that was of a vicarious nature. *Lutron* defines the price paid canceling our debt.[2]

A ransom is the amount that must be given in order to buy someone's freedom. Sin has brought mankind into bondage to self and Satan. The price that must be paid is that of the blood of an innocent person who, personally, owes no debt. The seriousness of our crime against God requires this great price. But because of the greatness and grace of our God, He pays the price Himself in the Person of Jesus.

Matthew 26:28 tells us that the blood of Jesus was poured out for the forgiveness of __*SIN*__.

John 1:7 says that the blood of Jesus purifies us from every __*SIN*__.

Because of the blood of Jesus, we come into right standing with God as if there had never been a problem. "Much more then, having now been justified by His blood, we shall be saved from wrath through Him" (Rom. 5:9).

WORD WEALTH

Justified, *dikaioo* (dik-ah-*yah*-oh); *Strong's #1344.* A legal term signifying to acquit, declare righteous, show to be righteous.[3] The idea is that we are so completely free in our restoration to God, it is as if we never sinned. The blood of Jesus has rendered us this free.

In what does Paul say we are justified? (1 Cor. 6:11)

NAME OF JESUS

By what is a person not justified? (Gal. 2:16)

NAME OF JESUS

(Rom. 10:9–10) That if you *SPEAK* with your mouth the Lord Jesus and *BELIEVE* in your heart that God raised Him from the dead, you will be saved.

Once we have received Christ, our desire should be that others come to know Him also. Of course, we cannot "save" a person ourselves. We cannot determine the moment someone else will truly come to know the Lord. This is the point Jesus is making when He says, "The wind blows where it wishes, and you hear the sound of it, but cannot tell where it comes from and where it goes. So is everyone who is born of the Spirit" (John 3:8). Our responsibility is simply to tell the good news. In doing so, however, be careful of two things:

1. Don't try to second-guess what the person's response should be because you will probably be disappointed. Just come to the conversation and minister the truth and life of Jesus, and let the Holy Spirit take it from there.

List some assumptions you may have brought to a conversation with a possible "convert" and why these may have led to disappointment; for example, the church they "need" to start attending.

THE UNDERSTAND THE IDEAS OF CHRISTIANITY

2. Try not to show disappointment if a person doesn't become a Christian right away.

List any unrealistic expectations you may have concerning a person's response to praying to receive Jesus.

EVERY PERSON WILL PRAY

There is perhaps no greater joy than seeing someone truly come to know Jesus. Consider carefully the following statement in light of winning the lost:

Living, vital, Holy Spirit-filled Christianity reaches people and often leads them to Christ.

In your own words define the following:

"Living" Christianity   *A PERSON PERSUING THE WILL OF GOD*

"Vital" Christianity

CHRIST IS THE CENTER OF A PERSON'S LIFE

"Holy Spirit-filled" Christianity

A PERSON ACTIVILY MOVING AND MINISTERING

DON'T OVERLOOK THESE

- *Recognize that the new birth process is multi-staged.* When we encounter people who are opening their hearts to Jesus Christ, we don't know where they are on the spectrum of God's dealings with them. But the Holy Spirit knows. Therefore it becomes necessary to rely on the Holy Spirit as we minister.

- *Invite the Holy Spirit to minister to them.* We need to minister with trust in God the Holy Spirit and listen to Him. In John 16 the Bible teaches that the Holy Spirit convicts people of sin. The Holy Spirit shows Jesus to them so clearly that they will know that only He can save them. The Holy Spirit also reveals that the power of sin has been broken, and that the serpent has been smashed and that the power of death and hell have been overcome. That's what Jesus meant when He said that when the Holy Spirit would come, He will convince the world of sin and righteousness and judgment.

- *Know the Word and believe in its power as we minister.* In John 6:63 Jesus says that the flesh profits nothing. We can bring all kinds of experience and wisdom to speaking with people, but what we bring naturally out of ourselves will lead no one to Christ. In contrast, the words that Jesus speaks are Spirit and life.

Know what the Bible says and trust the Holy Spirit to make it alive, and life, to people. Even if we see no response on a person's face, the Holy Spirit will take the Word as we speak it and accomplish His purposes.

THE SIMPLICITY OF THE PROCESS

1. *Focus on Jesus Himself as God's Son and resurrected Savior.*

Frequently you will find many questions and concerns that tend to draw attention away from a person's need to accept Jesus. Keep focused on the issue of new birth. Write out the five scriptures below. You may want to copy the references into the front of your Bible for future use.

When a person says:

a) I'm not sure that Jesus is the only way to be saved.
   Respond by quoting Acts 4:12:

b) I'm a good person, I don't hurt other people.
   Respond by quoting Rom. 3:23:

c) I'm not worried about what happens after I die.
Respond by quoting Rom. 6:23:

d) There are too many hypocrites in the church.
Respond by quoting John 21:22:

e) How do I know that God will accept me?
Respond by quoting John 1:12 and John 6:37:

Make a list of other potential questions and excuses people use to avoid the issue of salvation. Find appropriate scriptures with which to respond.

There will be times when questions arise for which you don't have answers. Be honest and admit that you don't know how to respond. If the person gives you time, suggest that you will find answers to their questions. Also, be careful that you don't become a Scripture "machine gun." You don't need to feel that everything you say is a quote from Scripture. People are looking for genuine, concerned, loving individuals who can carry on normal conversations without appearing to know everything and without appearing to be overly religious.

2. Present the promises of acceptance, forgiveness, assurance, and eternal life.
When we accept Christ we are fully accepted and entirely forgiven. That's what is offered to the person who comes to Jesus. Show the person you are witnessing to the scriptures that state the following truths. Write them out here, and, again, you may want to note the references in your Bible.

a) Acceptance (Eph. 1:6)

b) Forgiveness (Eph. 1:7)

c) Assurance (2 Tim. 3:14; Phil. 1:6; 1 John 3:19)

d) Eternal life (Rom. 6:23; 1 John 2:25)

3. Invite the seeker to prayer as an action of faith in God's promises. Show them that they can come to God and ask Him for forgiveness and salvation. Again, note these scriptures for reference.

a) Come (John 6:37)

b) Ask (John 16:24)

4. Help the person pray to receive Jesus. Below is a simple but to-the-point prayer that you may want to keep handy, or memorize in your own words, to use when necessary.

> Father God, I accept Jesus as my Savior and ask Him to come into my heart. Forgive me of my sins and cleanse me from all unrighteousness. Thank You that Jesus died on the Cross to save me from sin. Take control of my life. I surrender it to You right now.

Afterward, show them the following scriptures by way of assurance of their new life.

What does a person become upon receiving Jesus? (2 Cor. 5:17)

New Creation

What else does a person become upon receiving Jesus? (1 John 3:2)

Children of God

We pass from what to what upon receiving Jesus? (1 John 3:14)

Death to Life

5. *Affirm their obedience to God and say a prayer of thanksgiving:*

Father God, thank You that _____ (name) has surrendered his/her life to You by inviting Jesus to take up residence within their heart. Thank You that he/she has entered into eternal life and is now a child of God. We thank You that the blood of Jesus cleanses us from sin. Father, we also thank You that the Scripture affirms that You will work in us to bring us safely to heaven. May we be mindful of Your great grace and willingness to help us in every detail of our lives. Let us never forget Your Word and the assurance it brings to our hearts.

THEIR FIRST STEPS

New converts need to understand some important concepts and kingdom principles as soon as possible. Here are several. In each case let the Word of God do the convincing. We are called to share the Word, not force it on people.

- God will complete the work He started in us. (Phil. 1:6; 2:13)

- War is waging over the souls of men and women. (Luke 22:31; 1 Pet. 5:8; James 4:7; Eph. 6:10–12)

- God's Word provides protection, safety, and guidance. (Ps. 119:11, 105; Matt. 26:41)

- Christ's body, the church, is a corporate group for safety, comfort, fellowship, prayer, and sharing of burdens. (Gal. 6:2; Heb. 10:25; James 5:16)

New believers need to know that kingdom authority is available to them to be used against sin and Satan. The power of God, however, must not be sought or used for any reason other than the glorification of Jesus and the deliverance of people from bondage. Look carefully at Acts 8:14–24 and 19:11–20 to see what happens when motives are wrong.

FAITH ALIVE

Because of the price Jesus has paid to secure our release from sin, we are free from guilt and condemnation and have access directly to the throne of God. Such liberty, when fully understood, is the basis for a joy that is unspeakable.

Father in Heaven, I acknowledge the blood of Jesus that was poured out on Calvary to set me free from sin. I thank You that sin no longer holds me in bondage and that because of my release from it, I am also released from the power of Satan and his demons.

1. *Spirit-Filled Life Bible* (Nashville: Thomas Nelson Publishers, 1991), 1031, "Word Wealth: Is. 52:9 redeemed."

2. Ibid., 1444, "Word Wealth: Matt. 20:28 ransom."

3. Ibid., 1427, "Word Wealth: Matt. 12:37 justified."

Lesson 5/Where Are All the Evangelists?

My family and I were visiting old Olvera Street, "the birthplace of Los Angeles," during the Christmas season. At this time of the year the local merchants conduct the traditional Mexican festivities known as "Las Posadas." This includes a candlelight procession with Mexican costumes and traditional Mexican hymns depicting the journey of Mary and Joseph to Bethlehem.

The festivities end at a nearby public plaza where a traditional nativity scene is set up with life-size figures and animals. In front of the nativity is an ominous disclaimer, a sign stating that though this plaza and stage area are on public property, the nativity itself has been provided by a nonprofit organization to depict the religious character of the original settlers. It then notes that by the middle 1800s these "Catholic Christians" were overwhelmed by "Yankees and Chinese" and were never again in the majority.

I couldn't help but see that sign as a commentary on the religious nature of our entire country. As our nation works its way into the third century of its existence, many preachers and publishers rightly remind us of the "conspicuous Christian presence" in our country's *past*. But many thoughtful Christians will have to also acknowledge that biblical religion no longer has any monopoly on the spiritual horizon of our country's *present*.

Why? In over 200 years of religious liberty and freedom to preach the gospel, why have we not been more successful in evangelizing our "Jerusalem . . . Judea and Samaria," let alone the uttermost parts of the earth?

FAITH ALIVE

The Great Commission (Matt. 28:16–20) was given to several groups of people. The eleven disciples were there. Possibly this was the time when five hundred plus saw Him (1 Cor. 15:6). Finally, what Christ said on this occasion applies today to all believers.

Why did Jesus claim authority in heaven and earth? (Compare v. 18 with Eph. 6:12.)

HE HAD THE AUTHORITY

How did Christ's authority extend to nature and nations? (See Dan. 4:25; Matt. 8:23–27.)

HE CALLED ON THE CREATION OF ALL THINGS

Why is this important to those who would seek to carry out the evangelistic mandate?

WE MUST RECOGNIZE WHERE THE AUTHORITY COMES FROM

Based on Christ's claim to authority, what command did He issue? (v. 19)

MAKE DISCIPLES

What three-step process in disciple-making is given?

- MAKE DISCIPLES
- BAPTIZE
- TEACH

The commission is restated in Mark 16:15–18. What confirming signs were promised to accompany both the message and the messenger?

SIGNS & WONDERS

In Luke's account, the Great Commission (Luke 24:44–49) extends to "all nations." What was to happen in Jerusalem before the disciples began their mission?

FILLED W/ HS

What was to be the message of the commission? (24:47)

PREACH TO ALL NATIONS

John's account of the Great Commission (John 20:19–23) stresses the power they would need to continue the work which the Father had begun in the Son.

How did Christ impart to them His very own Spirit?

HE HAS BREATHED

This "pretaste of Pentecost" indicated that the power for service was in the person of the Holy Spirit. Yet, taking together Mark 16:15–16, Luke 24:45–49, and John 20:21–23, how will some nevertheless respond even to Spirit-empowered service?

WILL NOT RECEIVE

WHERE ARE ALL THE EVANGELISTS?

Church growth strategists suggest that a chief purpose of the church is to proclaim Christ, to persuade people to become His disciples and responsible, reproducing members of His church. If this is so, then a recent report that Protestantism is shrinking from two-thirds of the population of the United States to an estimated one-third by the end of the century is especially discouraging. These statistics go on the show that in the year 1900 there were twenty-seven churches for every 10,000 Americans. Today there are fewer than twelve. And eighty to eighty-five percent of those existing American churches are estimated to have plateaued or to be in decline!

For a country which was forged and built on religious principles, where have we failed? Realistically, we might better ask, "Where have we succeeded?"

Christianity is losing its strength because people are not being evangelized and equipped to win others. In an age of specialization many pastors are cultivating teaching ministries, counseling ministries, writing ministries, building ministries, but very few evangelistic ministries.

Is the day of evangelism past? Where are all the evangelists?

WORD WEALTH

The word **evangelism** does not actually occur in Scripture. The Greek word for *euangelion* ("gospel," "good news") is its root, and focuses on the actual *proclamation* of good news of any sort. However, the verb *euangelizo* ("to evangelize") is used over fifty times of believers who were *presenting* the good news of God's love through Jesus Christ with the intent of *persuading* men and women to repent and receive God's forgiveness. Early Christians spontaneously evangelized as they "chattered," "proclaimed," and "preached" the Good News everywhere!

While many evangelized, some seemed specially called, motivated, and equipped, and they had unusual success. These were called **evangelists** *(euangelistes)*, but not often: Acts 21:8, 2 Tim. 4:5, and Eph. 4:11–12.

PROBING THE DEPTHS

Evangelism Involves...

1. Information: The Greek word *euangelion* means "the proclamation of good news." In the Greek Septuagint of the Old Testament it might mean any good, positive or helpful news. In the New Testament it was used exclusively of the good news of salvation through Jesus Christ. (See Luke 4:18–19.)

Gospel designation: "The beginning of the gospel of Jesus Christ, the Son of God." Mark 1:1

Gospel definition: "Moreover, brethren, I declare to you the gospel which I preached to you, which also you received and in which you stand, by which also you are saved, if you hold fast that word which I preached to you—unless you believed in vain. For I delivered to you first of all that which I also received: that Christ died for our sins according to the Scriptures, and that He was buried, and that He rose again the third day according to the Scriptures" (1 Cor. 15:1–4).

2. Intent: The Greek verb *euangelizo* meant 1) to bring good news, to announce glad tidings; (2) *to persuade others of the good news and to trust Jesus to save them from their sins.* The early Christians were not content to convey information about Christ alone. They were intent, as ambassadors of Christ, to persuade others to be reconciled to God through Christ.

"Therefore those who were scattered went everywhere *preaching the word"* (Acts 8:4).

They returned to Jerusalem, *preaching:* "So when they had testified and *preached the word* of the Lord, *the gospel* in many villages of the Samaritans" (Acts 8:25).

". . . we implore you on Christ's behalf, be reconciled to God" (2 Cor. 5:20).

3. Individuals: The New Testament uses the Greek *euangelistes* three times to speak of the role, work, and office of an evangelist.

The role of an evangelist: "On the next day we who were Paul's companions departed and came to Caesarea, and entered the house of Philip the evangelist, who was one of the seven, and stayed with him" (Acts 21:8).

The work of an evangelist: "But you be watchful in all things, endure afflictions, do the work of an evangelist, fulfill your ministry" (2 Tim. 4:5).

The office of an evangelist: "And He Himself gave some to be apostles, some prophets, some evangelists, and some pastors and teachers, for the equipping of the saints for the work of ministry, for the edifying of the body of Christ . . ." (Eph. 4:11, 12).

The Bible tells us that when the task is great and the workers are few, we should pray that the Lord of the harvest would send forth laborers to gather in the harvest. Perhaps we are not praying enough! Or perhaps He is waiting for us to reconsider the biblical pattern and priorities for harvesting. While much is written regarding the function of evangelism, few evangelize, and little is written (or scripturally understood) concerning the biblical office of evangelist.

THE FIRST EVANGELIST

The first New Testament use of the Greek word *euangelistes* is found in Acts 21:8 and refers to the only biblical mention of an individual evangelist. Paul and his party, after returning from his third missionary tour, "entered the house of Philip the evangelist, who was one of the seven, and abode with him."

What leadership role did "Philip the evangelist" fill in the local church in Jerusalem? (Acts 6:1–7)

MISSIONARIES

List the three qualifications of spiritual character and maturity which commended Philip to his peers. (Acts 6:3)

GOOD REP. / FILLED W/ WISDOM
FILLED W/ HS

How would each of these qualities be important to anyone serving in spiritual leadership?

THE H.S. EMPOWERS US TO DO HIS WILL

How did the apostles affirm the people's choice? (Acts 6:6)

LAID HANDS & ANOINTED

What were the results of restructuring ministry leadership more consistently with their spiritual gifts and motivations? (6:7)

MANY BELIEVED

After the stoning of Stephen (Acts 6:8—7:60), the church in Jerusalem faced increased persecution so severe that many Christians were scattered into Judea and Samaria. As the believers fled they went everywhere evangelizing *(euggelizomenoi)*, preaching the good news about Jesus Christ (Acts 8:4). An example of this preaching is found in Philip's "power encounter" evangelism. (Acts 8:6–8.)

How would you explain the miracles which were manifested? (See Mark 16:17 and 1 Cor. 12:9.) *H. S.*

What was the purpose for the apostles in Jerusalem to send Peter and John to Samaria?

TEACHING & SEEING MIRACLES

What do you think Simon "saw" when the apostles laid their hands on the new believers and prayed that they would "receive the Holy Spirit"?

MIRICLES

What did the two apostles do in several Samaritan villages before returning to Jerusalem? (Acts 8:25, *euangelizonto*)

MIRICLES

Later, Philip obeyed the Lord and went south into the desert for a divine appointment with the Ethiopian eunuch. After being supernaturally transported by the Spirit of the Lord to the coastal city of Azotus, Philip continued to evangelize in all the cities on his way to Caesarea, where he evidently relocated his family and home. Several years later he was to host the apostle Paul in his home in Caesarea (Acts 21:8). There is no indication that Philip continued any "mobile ministry."

What occurred to cause Philip to leave the comfort of Jerusalem and proclaim Christ to the Samaritans? (Acts 8:1–5)

PERSECUTION

How can we use negative situations as occasions to positively preach or proclaim the word of God concerning Christ?

GOD IS GREATER

What was the informational content of the "good news" Philip proclaimed? (Acts 8:6, 12, 35, 40.)

JOY OF GOD

How did the demonstration of God's power over disease and demons enhance the effectiveness of his evangelistic presentations? (Acts 8:6–8, 13.)

PEOPLE WANT TO BE DELIVERED

Is this kind of "signs and wonders" evangelism effective today?

YES

Philip was not only a "worker of miracles" but also a discipler. How did water baptism fit into his efforts of discipleship? (Acts 8:12, 16, 36–38.)

GOD CALLS US TO DO THIS

 KINGDOM EXTRA

Philip's life and ministry reveal characteristics for today's commission to make disciples for the King of kings. Not only was Philip a dedicated layman and a bold proclaimer of the gospel, he had the following traits:

- He was sensitive to God's prompting (Acts 8:26–27).
- He was available for eternal purposes (Acts 8:27–28).
- He used initiative to guide the conversation to spiritual truth (Acts 8:29–31).
- He was tactful and remained inoffensive (Acts 8:32–34).
- The message of the Cross may offend some, but the messenger should not.
- He was precise (Acts 8:34–35). He preached Jesus, not religion. He taught the Scripture, not opinions.
- He was decisive (Acts 8:36–39). Baptism is external evidence of inward work. It is a significant step of discipleship.

THE WORK OF AN EVANGELIST

The second place where the term evangelist is used in Scripture is 2 Timothy 4:5. Here Paul urges Timothy, whom he had left in Ephesus, to do several things. Among them: the work of an evangelist. The meaning of this phrase is dependent upon one's understanding of what role or office Timothy held. If he were a *traveling evangelist,* this admonition would seem inconsistent with Paul's earlier urging to "remain still in Ephesus." If he were a *young pastor,* as is often suggested, then Paul might be urging him to preach more evangelistically. If he were a *bishop (an overseer),* then he might be wanting Timothy to provide an evangelistic example and stimulus to the pastors under him.

However, in Paul's letter to the Thessalonians he seems to make it clear that whatever else Timothy may have been, he was also an apostle. Paul greeted the church on behalf of himself and "Silvanus and Timotheus" (1 Thess. 1:1), whom he later calls "apostles of Christ" (1 Thess. 2:6). The word *apostle* means "sent one." We know that there were twelve apostles chosen and sent out by Christ. There are also many apostles specifically named as having been chosen and sent out by local churches (Rom. 16:17; 1 Thess. 1:1; 2:6). We have already noted that disciples and apostles "evangelized," but Timothy is told to "do the work of an evangelist." Paul did not say "go evangelize," but rather to "do the *work* of an evangelist."

◤ FAITH ALIVE

Instead of evangelizing others, many churches concentrate on entertaining themselves. Ralph Neighbor estimates an average church spends over 300 hours a year equipping members for Christian service inside the church walls (choir practices, committee meetings, services, and so on). However, he says, "The average church does not provide as much as twelve hours a year to equip Christians to witness for Christ outside the church walls!"[1]

THE OFFICE OF EVANGELIST

The "work of an evangelist" may best be understood by observing the object of the office of evangelist, according to Ephesians 4:11 and 12, the third use of this word:

> And he gave some, apostles; and some, prophets; and some, evangelists; and some, pastors and teachers; for [*pros*] the perfecting of the saints, for [*eis*] the work of the ministry, for [*eis*] the edifying of the body of Christ.

The above is how the passage reads in the familiar King James version, with important Greek prepositions noted in brackets.

As James Kennedy, noted pastor and leader in evangelism, explains, "Instead of the preposition 'for' being repeated three times [in these verses], the Greek says *pros, eis,* and *eis,* which would be better rendered 'for,' 'unto,' 'unto.'"

AT A GLANCE: Ephesians 4:11 and 12

Christ established certain leadership roles or offices "for" the purpose of perfecting (equipping) the saints "unto" ministry.

The office	The object of the office
Apostles	To provide foundational strength and stability to the larger body of Christ.
Prophets	To edify, exhort, and comfort the church
Evangelists	To motivate the saints for the work of evangelism
Pastors	To lead, feed, and protect the flock of God
Teachers	To instruct the saints for spiritual growth and service

This familiar passage teaches that Christ established certain leadership roles or offices "for" the purpose of "perfecting" or "equipping" the saints: 1) "unto" the work of ministry (spiritual service), and 2) "unto" the upbuilding of the body of Christ.

This probably explains what Paul meant when he told Timothy to "do the work of an evangelist." He was to equip, train, and motivate the saints to "proclaim the Good News."

What role in evangelism do all Christians share in common? (Acts 1:8) *THE H.S. GIVES US POWER TO BE WITNESSES*

What mutual ministry do all believers have? (2 Cor. 5:18) *BOTH G WITNESSES*

What enables believers to serve the Lord and others in special ways? (See 1 Peter 4:10 and 1 Cor. 12:4–7) *THE POWER OF THE HS*

BEHIND THE SCENES

Christ has placed certain saints into leadership roles to equip and enable the body to accomplish His purposes in the world. The *pastor* personally witnesses, but publicly *feeds* the saints. The *teacher* personally witnesses, but publicly *instructs* the saints. The *evangelist* personally witnesses, *possibly with greater conviction, confidence, and compulsion* than others (I Cor. 12:4–11), but publicly, within the body, he *motivates* the saints for evangelism. Rather than being a competitor, the evangelist actually complements the ministry of the pastor. Indeed, some feel every congregation should have someone who has the special ministry of motivating and equipping believers for the work of evangelism.

EQUIPPING THE SAINTS

As we have already noted, a primary object of the evangelist is meant to be to the saints. This is perhaps the greatest difference between the early church and today. Early evangelists seem to have had a deep concern to train the saints to be witnesses.

Robert Schuller, well-known founder-pastor of the Crystal Cathedral in Garden Grove, has said, "The first person added to our staff was the Minister of Evangelism. His job description was and is today: 'To recruit, train, and motivate laymen and laywomen to be lay evangelists of the church.'"[2] While there are many fine evangelical churches in and around Garden Grove, Schuller and his fellow ministers and lay evangelists pray and plan as if they were the only church to reach the hundreds of thousands of unchurched people who live within fifteen minutes of their location. As a result, over 1,000 unchurched people are being won into a lively membership of this church each year.

Jesus said, "I will build My Church." Upon His ascension to heaven, "He gave some to be . . . evangelists . . . for the equipping of the saints [unto] the work of the ministry [unto] the upbuilding of the body of Christ." Leighton Ford reiterates this thought when he says that "the evangelist is to evangelize and also to equip others to evangelize. As he evangelizes, he communicates something of his own passion and 'know-how' to his co-workers."[3]

The professional evangelist undoubtedly has a place in God's workings today. His enthusiasm and example can stir the saint to revival and the sinner to repentance by his prophetic utterances from the pulpit.

But the unfinished task of evangelizing the lost is still a fantasy unless we can motivate and mobilize evangelists in every church to equip the saints of their church for ministry to those outside the body who will never attend an evangelistic crusade, or read the evangelist's monthly magazine, or watch his television specials. It is not "either/or" but "both/and." The task is too great to leave to the relatively few "mobile ministries."

BEHIND THE SCENES

Demographic strategists remind us that within our fifty states there are 224 major metropolitan areas. Also, there are some 176,000 political precincts. Political parties know that if they are to influence the electorate they must successfully "work the precincts" among the "grass roots."

FAITH ALIVE

George W. Peters believes that "as we mobilize the church in evangelism, we will soon discover that a three-winged pattern will evolve. In general, we will find that some ten to fifteen percent can be mobilized for active confrontational evangelism. An additional twenty to thirty percent can be trained in friendship evangelism. The remainder must be trained in prayer evangelism, prayer which undergirds the other two efforts. Thus the total church becomes involved."[4]

MULTIPLICATION

If a church were to motivate and mobilize just ten percent of its members for effective evangelism, and if they won just one soul per year each, that congregation would double in less than a decade. If those converts were nurtured and discipled and ten percent of them joined the other "witnesses" in winning one soul to Christ per year, that church would more than triple in twelve years!

What would happen for the Kingdom of God's sake if hundreds of churches in major metropolitan areas were to carefully consider those among them who were evangelistically motivated and successful? And what if they were to encourage them in their ministries and provide financially for them so they could give themselves to "equip the saints unto the work of the ministry" of evangelism?

Or consider the possible effect of just one gifted man or woman accurately and actively fulfilling the biblical role of evangelist (as suggested above) in each of the 176,000 political precincts across America. Can you begin to smell the fires of revival? Jesus said, "The harvest truly is great, but the laborers are few: pray ye therefore the Lord of the harvest, that he would send forth laborers into his harvest." (Luke 10:2). We are to be either the laborers or the prayers!

We must remember that Christ is still giving evangelists to the church to equip the saints (Eph. 4:11, 12). We must seek to *recognize* those evangelists and *release* them to the ministry God has intended, that "all men should come to *repentance*."

1. Ralph Neighbor, *The Seven Last Words of the Church* (Grand Rapids, Mich.: Zondervan Publishing, 1973), 57.

2. Robert H. Shuller, *Your Church Has Real Possibilities* (Ventura, Calif.: Regal Books, 1974), 64.

3. Leighton Ford, Carl F. Henry, eds., *One Race, One Gospel, One Task* (Minneapolis, Minn.: World Wide Publications, 1967), 467.

4. George W. Peters, Paul E. Little, eds., *Reaching All* (Minneapolis, Minn.: World Wide Publications, 1974), 202.

Lesson 6/ Under the King's Call

The Gospels proclaim the good news of the coming Kingdom of God. They share God's global goal to rule and reign as King in the lives of the redeemed.

 BEHIND THE SCENES

Mark shows Jesus to be a servant, who came "not to be served, but to serve, and to give His life a ransom for many" (10:45). Luke shows the universality of the Christian message by presenting Jesus as the Savior of the world. The focus is on Jesus, the Prophet, whose role becomes equated with Matthew's Messiah and Mark's Servant (see Luke 4:24; 7:16, 39; 9:19; 24:19). John presents a more focused study of Jesus as the only begotten Son of God who became flesh that he might reveal the Father and redeem the fallen. "By believing that Jesus is the Christ, the readers of John's Gospel became participants in the life Jesus brought out of death (20:31)."[1]

THE KINGDOM INTRODUCED

Matthew presents Jesus as the King of Israel, in fulfillment of the Old Testament promises concerning the Messiah. His Gospel gives the church its "clarion call to mission, the proclamation of the good news to all peoples."[2]

The term "kingdom of God" or "kingdom of heaven" occurs over 120 times in the synoptic Gospels (Matthew, Mark, and

Luke, which are best understood when "viewed together"; thus the term "syn-optic"). The term "kingdom" is used fifty times in Matthew, twenty-two times in Mark, and forty-four times in Luke. Each time it emphasizes God's rule as King. Its context must decide whether it is speaking about:

- The realm or territory that is ruled
- The people over which a monarch reigns/rules, both present and future
- The reign or rule of the monarch.

Review the context of each of the scriptures below and then indicate whether the use of the word "kingdom" is referring to the realm, the people, or the reign of the king.

Matthew	4:8	*REALM*
	6:13	*REALM*
	6:33	*REALM*
	11:12	*REALM*
	19:23–24	*REALM*
	24:7	*REALM*
Mark	10:15	*REALM*
	12:34	*REALM*
Luke	4:5	*REALM*
	19:12	*REALM*
	16:16	*REALM*
	22:29	*REALM*
1 Cor.	15:24–26	*REALM*
Col.	1:13	*REALM*

KINGDOM EXTRA

Matthew 19:23 and 24 uses the phrases "kingdom of heaven" and "kingdom of God" interchangeably. In doing so, it sufficiently demonstrates that the two terms are meant to refer to one and the same thing: the kingdom. Although some make a labored distinction between them, this text and ten others in the Gospels clearly show that the "kingdom of heaven" and "kingdom of God" are verifiably synonyms. Matthew is the only New Testament writer who used the term "kingdom of heaven." Doing so, he showed a sensitivity toward his originally intended audience of Jewish readers, for whom too frequent a use of the name of "God" would have seemed irreverent. By a variety of terms, Matthew refers to "the kingdom" fifty times in his Gospel: thirty-two times as "kingdom of heaven"; five times as "kingdom of God"; four times as kingdom of "the Son of Man." The remaining nine references are simply to "the kingdom" without other designation. This variety in the usage, made by the only one using the phrase "kingdom of heaven," surely shows these terms to be synonyms for the kingdom.[3]

THE KINGDOM EXPRESSED

The Sermon on the Mount expressed the internal attitudes as well as the outward actions of a citizen of the kingdom. It pictures a truly righteous person and reveals his actions and attitudes in relationship to a myriad of relationships. By studying the sermon (Matt. 5—7; Luke 6) we learn kingdom wisdom regarding sin, worship, wealth, hypocritical judgments, false prophets, and God's will.

Read the following references and write a summary statement about each one.

Matt. 5:1–16 *BEATITUDES*

Matt. 5:21–48 *ATTITUDE OF HEART*

Matt. 6:1–18 *PRAYER Y PLEASING GOD*

Matt. 6:19–34 *SERVE GOD RATHER THAN MAN*

Matt. 7:1–12 *DONT JUDGE BUT RIGHTOUS*

Matt. 7:13–20 *THE ROAD IS NARROW, BEAR FRUIT*

Matt. 7:21–29 *PUT YOUR FOUNDATION ON GOD*

Do you believe the demands of the Sermon on the Mount to be more or less difficult than those found in the Law of Moses? Why? *EQUAL, THE LAW OF MOSES IS LAW, SERMON IS THE WAY WE SHOULD LIVE*

How does Paul explain putting the Sermon on the Mount into practice in Romans 8:1–4? *WE ARE FREED FROM THE CONDEMNATION OF SIN*

KINGDOM EXTRA

In the Sermon on the Mount, Jesus outlines the primary attributes of people who receive the rule of the kingdom He brings. Nine direct references to "the kingdom" are in this sermon, calling for: humility (5:3), willingness to suffer persecution (5:10), earnest attention to God's commandments (5:19), refusal to substitute false piety for genuinely right behavior (5:20), a life of prayer (6:10, 13), prioritizing spiritual over material values (6:33), and above all, acknowledging Christ's lordship by obeying the revealed will of God (7:21). Clearly the authority Christ hopes to delegate to His own is intended to be exercised by disciples willing to accept renewal in soul and behavior, as well as rebirth through forgiveness of sin. To these, obviously, the call to "kingdom" living and ministry includes the expectation that Holy Spirit-begotten fruit and gifts will develop in the believer. The same Spirit that distributes gifts of power for kingdom service also works in us to beget kingly qualities of life, love, and a holy character (John 15:1–17; Gal. 5:22, 23).[4]

THE KINGDOM MESSAGE

Jesus spoke many parables. They were used most frequently to convey truths connected with the subject of the kingdom of God. The Greek word for "parable" is *parabole* and meant something thrown alongside another for comparison. A parable was a comparison drawn from nature or daily life, designed to teach some spiritual truth.

How regularly did Jesus incorporate parables into His teachings? (Matt. 13:10, 34)

MANY MANY TIMES

Why do you think he used these "earthly stories with heavenly meanings"?

TO BRING UNDERSTAND

Did the disciples find the parables easy or difficult to understand?

DIFFICULT

His disciples asked (v. 10) why He used hard-to-understand illustrations. He explained that it was to fulfill prophecy (v. 35) and to keep the unbelieving from becoming even more guilty for rejecting the King and His kingdom (v. 11). Only His disciples, who were spiritually responsive and sensitive, were permitted to understand these "mysteries" or sacred secrets about the kingdom (see vv. 18, 36, 37).

As you study the parables, are you a skeptical onlooker or a sincere disciple? *DISCIPLE*

As you come across hard-to-understand sections of Scripture, do you pray for understanding? The psalmist David did. Read his prayers in Psalm 119:9–12, 17–19, 25–27, and 33–34. Write out your own prayer:

THE PARABLE OF THE SOILS

The parable in Matthew 13:1–23 tells about a farmer who goes out into his field to sow precious seed. The custom was to dip into a sack and "broadcast" the seed all around.

According to verses 4–8, on how many different kinds of soil did the seed fall? *4*

What happened to the seed that fell on each kind of soil?

- Pathway – *BIRDS ATE IT*
- Rocky Soil – *SPRUNG UP QUICK BUT DIED QUICK*
- Among Thorns – *CHOCKED BY THORNS*
- Good Soil – *HEALTHY & BORE FRUIT*

The seed that fell on the pathway was stolen and eaten by birds. It had no chance to grow or bear fruit for the farmer.

The seed in rocky soil fell into a stony subsurface that had a shallow layer of earth over it. When the seed sprang to life, it soon withered away because it had no deep root. Consequently, no fruit!

Other seed fell among thorns and was strangled by the thorns before it had a chance to bear fruit.

Finally, some seed fell on good soil. It bore a rich harvest for the farmer, but even then it was uncertain and unpredictable. Some areas yielded thirtyfold increase, some sixty and even some one hundred times as much as had been planted.

FAITH ALIVE

As a devoted disciple, you need to see yourself as a sower of the precious seed of the gospel. You are well aware that different individuals will respond differently to the Word sown.

Some seem to reject it as quickly as it is spoken. Like Jesus explained in verse 19, "Satan comes and snatches away the seeds from his heart." In other lives, there seems to be some growth, but it turns out to be shallow, and what looked promising one week is withered the next. Others seem distracted by home and personal problems, and what was meant to grow got strangled.

Then there is the good ground! God has been sovereignly working to prepare that soil. Rocky subsurfaces have been broken up, thorns removed, pathways plowed under, and the Word of God roots deeply and returns a full harvest. Praise God!

What is our job in this great kingdom harvest? We are to sow! We don't know which seed will grow. We don't know which life will respond to our message and ministry. That is up to God. We are just to be faithful sowers of the Word.

THE PARABLE OF THE WHEAT AND WEEDS

A parable in Matthew 13:24–30 and 36–41 shows that good seed does not grow uncontested. The enemy is working alongside our efforts. This may cause us to become discouraged and cynical of our results. Consider this pessimistic poem:

> God's Word made a hopeful beginning;
> Man spoiled the creation by sinning;
> We know that the story
> Will end in God's glory,
> But at present the other side's winning!

Sometimes the reality of the old and the new natures working in the lives of those we are discipling is too much for us! Some seem so promising, but then we find that though there has been progress in their lives, there certainly is not perfection!

 FAITH ALIVE

What are we to do? Whatever it is, it must be done carefully. We don't want to hurt the wheat while trying to take care of the weeds! The best thing may be to pray for such believers. There is an enemy contesting for their souls. God is even more interested in their spiritual progress than we are. Trust Him!

THE PARABLE OF THE SEED AND YEAST

The parable in Matthew 13:31–33 is one of hope and encouragement, of reassurance and promise. It speaks of the outward growth we can expect as well as the inward growth for which we must trust God.

The parable speaks of the *potential for growth* in the mustard seed. It is tiny. It is almost "insignificant." But later it can grow into a huge tree, where even birds can come and find shelter. How does this happen? We don't know. We don't accomplish it. God does. We are to plant, water, and cultivate it. God will give the increase. The kingdom may grow slowly, secretly, but it will surely grow.

In verse 33, the parable speaks of the *power of permeation.* The woman mixes yeast into the flour and before long it has affected the whole batch of dough. By itself it, too, seemed insignificant and useless. Mixed with the right material, it transformed the "measure" into a full meal!

 FAITH ALIVE

Again, we must *trust God to transform* our "insignificant" efforts into something larger than ourselves. We can barely imagine how God can multiply our small efforts. Consider the following:

- A Sunday school teacher, a Mr. Kimball, in 1858 led a Chicago shoe clerk to Christ.
- The clerk, Dwight L. Moody, became an evangelist. In England in 1879, he awakened evangelistic zeal in the heart of Frederick B. Meyer, pastor of a small church.
- F.B. Meyer, preaching on an American college campus, brought a student named J. Wilbur Chapman to Christ.
- Chapman, engaged in YMCA work, employed a former baseball player, Billy Sunday, to do evangelistic work.
- Billy Sunday held a revival in Charlotte, North Carolina. A group of local men were so enthusiastic afterward that they planned another evangelistic campaign, bringing Mordecai Ham to town to preach.
- During Ham's revival, a young man named William Graham heard the gospel and yielded his life to Christ.
- It may be that *you* are one of the tens of thousands who have been affected by the ministry of Billy Graham!

Only eternity will reveal the tremendous impact of that one Sunday School teacher who invested his life in the lives of others. The parable of the seed and the yeast challenges us to *trust God to transform* our present insignificant efforts into something far-reaching later.

THE KINGDOM'S REJECTION

Jesus' triumphal entry into Jerusalem (Matt. 21 and Mark 11), the Sunday before His crucifixion and resurrection, was a prophetic action which fulfilled the prophecy of Zechariah 9:9. Because He was the prophetic "King," His excited subjects paid homage and sang "hosanna." They praised him as the awaited Messiah by crying out Psalm 118:26: "Blessed is he who comes in the name of the Lord!" However, they overlooked verses 22–23, "The stone which the builders rejected has become the chief cornerstone. This was the Lord's doing; it is marvelous in our eyes."

Jesus quoted this verse later (Matt. 21:42), when he told the parable of the wicked vinedressers. At that time, it was obvious to the Pharisees that Jesus was speaking of them, and they "sought to lay hands on Him," but they hesitated because the multitude perceived Him to be a prophet.

Jesus warned the religious rulers about rejecting Him by teaching three parables. Some have called these the parables of rejection. Review the parables and summarize the teaching below.

The two sons (Matt. 21:28–32)

- WORKING IN THE VINEYARD
- WHICH SON WAS RIGHT

The wicked husbandmen (21:33–41)

THE SON WAS REJECTED

The marriage of the king's son (22:1–14)

THE CHOSEN REJECTED
SO THE INVITATION WAS OPEN

In rejecting Jesus they rejected the kingdom He offered. As a result, what is to happen to "the kingdom of God"? (Matt. 21:43)

OPEN TO ALL

Who do you think the other "nation" is in Matthew 22:43, which will give God the appropriate fruit He desires?

THE SPIRIT FILLED WITNESS

Is this a reference meaning that God will include Gentiles in His plan for gospel globalization?

YES

In the parable of the bridegroom (Matt. 22:1–14), what happened to the city whose people rejected the wedding invitation? How does that predict the destruction of Jerusalem?

THE KING'S CALL

The King concluded His earthly ministry by calling His disciples to extend His Lordship to "all the nations" (Greek *ethne*). This "Great Commission" to world evangelism is passed on to all disciples to the "end of the age."

What contrasts and similarities can you find in the Great Commission, as given in Matthew (28:18–20) and Mark (Mark 16:15–18, 20)?

The Matthew commission:

- AUTHORITY
- MAKE DISCIPLES
- BAPTIZE
- TEACH

GOD IS WITH US ALWAYS

The Mark commission:

- GO INTO ALL THE WORLD
- PREACH
- BAPTIZE
- SIGNS
- SPEAK W/OTHER TONGUES

THEY WENT

KINGDOM EXTRA

Since Matthew's theme is Christ as King, it is unsurprising Jesus' final commission to His disciples reflects His global perspective. In teaching kingdom life and principles ("kingdom" appears over fifty times in Matthew), Jesus leads His followers to think, live, and pray that His kingdom come to our entire planet (6:10). In chapter 13, His parables illustrated the kingdom's global expansion (v. 33). As His disciples began to minister, He told them to preach *everywhere:* "The kingdom of God is at hand." Then, before His ascension, the King gave the Great Commission. This climaxing command to go to all nations directed that their teaching and preaching seek to bring all nations into His kingdom (28:18–20). Prophetically, He forecast that the end would come only as "this gospel of the kingdom" was preached "in all the world as a witness to all nations" (24:14). "Nations" (Greek *ethne*) means "people groupings"—today, about 22,000 on this globe.[5]

1. *Spirit-Filled Life Bible* (Nashville: Thomas Nelson Publishers, 1991), 1572, "Christ Revealed."
2. Ibid., 1402, "Personal Application."
3. Ibid., 1442, "Kingdom Dynamics: Matt. 19:23, 24, Synonymous Expressions."
4. Ibid., 1410, "Kingdom Dynamics: Matt. 5:1—7:27, Basic Traits."
5. Ibid., 1464, "Kingdom Dynamics: Matt. 28:18–20, Commissioned Under the King's Call."

Lesson 7 / Compelled by Compassion

Without dwelling on the word too long, get a picture in your mind that illustrates "evangelism."

Was your mental image of evangelism anything like:

- A man passing out tracts on a street corner?
- A missionary doctor sharing Jesus with tribal natives?
- A televangelist with a Bible?
- Jesus preaching from a boat?
- A revival meeting at your church?

Maybe you had a totally different image; for example:

- Two men eating lunch at a business convention.
- A travel agent enjoying afternoon tea with a famous actress?
- Two cable splicers hoisted up high on a telephone pole by a hydraulic lift, conversing in the noonday sun.

Most readers probably imagined images like the first five. After all, those are evangelistic settings, right? We'd probably call those "spiritual," or "sacred" in contexts: the church, the revival meeting, the missionary doctor.

In contrast, we'd probably call the other three settings "secular": an executive luncheon, tea with an actress, sweating over high-power lines. We usually think there's nothing "spiritual," or "sacred" in those scenarios, unless those people were talking about the Good News of Jesus Christ!

Interesting concept, though false. Jesus Himself ignored the labels of "secular" and "sacred," because *any place* He went became sacred. In reaching out to sinners, He personalized the gospel to each individual, speaking in terms the world understood, wherever He met them. So did the apostles. Paul, preaching his sermon to the Greeks on Mars Hill, is a great example.

LOOKING AT LUKE

Luke, the beloved physician, wrote one of the most "sacred" books ever written. Yet he prefaces his story in a most unreligious manner, avoiding religious clichés. Instead, he sounds more like a secular historian. In fact, Luke wrote in a formal style of Greek, such as one would find in the work of a secular writer. He was addressing the world at large, claiming a place for Christianity on the stage of world history.

Luke, however, didn't speak to the world *on* its terms, but *in* its terms. He was linguistically sensitive to nonbelievers.

In so doing, he did not pollute the gospel, he clarified it.

He did not mystify or spiritualize Jesus; he made Him touchable for ordinary people. He did not blind nonbelievers with mysterious language; he made the message and story easy to understand. Such an approach stimulates interest among ordinary nonbelievers.

As a result, Luke's Gospel has been studied in a myriad of secular university classrooms. They appreciate its literary excellence, and the message has been heard by people who would likely not step inside a church.

Probably no other book of the New Testament could serve as a text on world evangelism in quite the same way as Luke's Gospel. Born a Greek, Luke was the only Gentile writer of the New Testament. This gave him a special evangelistic inclination toward the Gentile world.

Perhaps that telephone cable-splicer, sweating in the heat of the day as he shared his faith with his crusty co-worker, found a listening ear because he genuinely cared for the man, had an orderly account ready to share, and spoke the language of his listener—true to Luke's style.

THE BIRTH OF THE MESSAGE

The Good News we share with the world is a Person: the Source of Eternal Life, the Savior, Lord, Healer, King, Creator, and Redeemer—not to mention Wonderful, Counselor, Mighty God, Everlasting Father, Prince of Peace, Good Shepherd, Son of David, the Seed of Woman, the Son of Man, the Son of God. The list goes on and on. He's so vast and glorious, it takes a galaxy of titles even to begin to describe the Person we preach.

> Yet, the Infinite God became finite;
> the Creator became the created;
> the ultimate Voice of hope for Mankind began with a newborn baby's cry.

 PROBING THE DEPTHS

Luke's Gospel gives us the account of God coming to earth. Fill in the blanks as you refer to the first chapter of Luke:

- From earth's view of things, where was the glorious event of the Incarnation to take place? (1:26) _NAZARETH_ .
- Who was the very first person to receive this Good News? (1:27) _VIRGIN MARY_ .
- Verse 31 says: "And behold, you will _CONCEIVE_ in your _womb_ and _BRING_ _FORTH_ a _CHILD_, and shall call His _NAME JESUS_."
- According to Genesis 3:15, Jehovah God planned to redeem mankind from the curse of the Fall by using the Seed of a _WOMAN_ .
- The fulfillment of that promise is described in Luke 1:35, where it says "the _POWER_ of the _HIGHEST_ will _OVERSHADOW_ you; therefore, also, that Holy One _WHO_ _IS_ _TO_ _BE_ _BORN_ will be called the Son of God."

Thus, God's blueprint for the redemption of mankind would be that His Son would be born human flesh and blood.

MORE THAN A PROUD MOTHER

In Luke 1:46–55, Mary has arrived at Elizabeth's house and is sharing the good news about the Savior's imminent birth. She breaks forth into song, ecstatic over the news that she is to be mother of the Messiah. This miracle brings an avalanche of praise from her lips, extolling God for His goodness to all who trust in

Him. Review Mary's song and list four phrases that are reasons why she is proclaiming the Good News.

1. *HE HAS REGARDED HER*

2. *HE WHO IS MIGHTY HAS DONE GREAT THINGS*

3. *MERCY ON THOSE WHO FEAR HIM*

4. *HE HAS FILLED THE HUNGRY WITH GOOD THINGS*

The Holy Spirit's coming upon Mary in Nazareth provided a miraculous conception, unprecedented in history. The baby in Mary's womb experienced a normal gestation period, but beyond that, was unique in every way! Out of the four Gospels, Luke is the only one that traces Jesus' lineage all the way back to Adam, back to the first generation where God uttered the original promise of a Redeemer. He said in Genesis 3:15 that salvation will come through the Seed of woman.

Christ, being God and a sinless human being, was able to die for the sins of others. He totally identified with humanity by becoming one of us and facing all the various kinds of temptations we have faced, yet without sin.

This process of intimate identification with humanity is an underlying theme in Luke. As we noted previously, Luke's genealogy stretches back to Adam, but Luke repeats the reference the "Son of Man" nearly twice as many times as John and Mark, and close to the number of times as Matthew. This name was how Christ often referred to Himself. "For the Son of Man came to seek and to save that which was lost" (Luke 19:10). The purpose of Jesus becoming the "Son of Man" is stated in that verse, a statement of world evangelism if ever there was one. Because, by using this term, "Son of Man," Jesus could disclose His Messiahship to those who welcomed it, while to those resisting His claims, He obscured it. The listener made the choice; Jesus didn't force the issue.

Also by that term, Jesus related Himself to both God and mankind, showing the beauty and uniqueness of both His humanity and divinity in perfect symmetry.

✎ WORD WEALTH

Son, *ben (behn); Strong's #1121.* A son, a child. The plural is not restricted to the meaning "sons," but often means "children" or "descendants" of both genders. An example is the phrase *b'nay yisrael* (literally, "sons of Israel"), generally translated "children of Israel." The root from which *ben* comes is possibly *banah,* meaning "to build up," or "to fortify." The idea is that a son is a builder of future generations.[1]

BUILDING FUTURE GENERATIONS

Jesus as the Son of Man is "a builder of future generations." In so doing, He begets sons (John 1:12) who also build future generations. Beyond the physical reality of procreation we are builders of future spiritual generations through the effective sharing of our faith. As spiritual sons or seeds of Abraham (Rom. 4:16) we propagate the spiritual lineage through the testimony of our faith. It is only through Jesus, the Seed of Father Abraham, that the continuation of eternal life-giving faith can pass on to others.

 FAITH ALIVE

After being commissioned into ministry at His baptism, Jesus was led by the Spirit into the wilderness, where He was severely tempted by the devil.

Can any of us identify with that process? Have you ever had a major move of God in your life when, wham! the forces of hell shot their arsenal at you! "What's this? I just had the glory of God come down! Now I'm in the furnace of affliction!"

How do you evaluate the temptations of Jesus? Were they real or imagined? Were they difficult, or, since He was God, did they not even cause Him to blink?

Jesus' temptations involved real-life areas of human conflict. Name three areas in which you are most often tempted. Can you find one scripture to answer each personal temptation the way Jesus did?

Review the temptation passage in Luke 4:1–13 and answer the following questions:

Why was it necessary for Jesus to be tempted? (See Hebrews 2:17.) *IN ALL THINGS HE HAD TO BE MADE LIKE HIS BRETHERN*

Can you categorize the main areas of human experience in which Jesus was tempted and relate them to your own experience?

PRIDE
SELFISHNESS
LUST

How did Jesus consistently respond to those temptations?

SCRIPTURE / AUTHORITY

KINGDOM EXTRA

Skim through the Gospel of Luke and list incidents that portray the evangelizing of these groups:

Gentiles *CENTURIANS SERVANT HEALD*

Samaritans *SAMARITAN WOMAN @ THE WELL*

Women - *VIRGIN MARY, WOMAN @ WELL*

Children *THE CHILDREN CAME TO JESUS JESUS HEALED MANY CHILDREN*

Sinners- *EVERYONE JESUS MINISTERED TO*

Outcasts *HEALD DEMONIAK & OTHERS PARALITIC HEALD*

What you've found are incidents of the sin-sick, suffering, brokenhearted, mistreated, and bereaved coming to Jesus, who has His arms outstretched, open to all.

A COMMISSION WITH COMPASSION

Now let's look at several scriptures about being commissioned with compassion. Answer each of the following questions with a few sentences about changing or improving how you relate to unsaved people.

What is the most important ingredient that needs to be present with our preaching of the Gospel? (Luke 10:30–36) How could you improve in this area?

LOVE, YIELD TO GOD'S LOVE WORKING THROUGH ME

How was Jesus always seeking to communicate His message to a lost world? (Luke 13:18–21) How could you improve in this respect?

PARABLES / STORIES

LET GOD USE ME TO HELP ILLUSTRATE HIS MESSAGE IN A BETTER WAY

What kind of people did Jesus feel were ready for the kingdom of God? (Luke 18:10–14) Do you associate with such people often?

THE LOWLY & HUMBLE

Did Jesus ever communicate that there was a cost in following Him? (Luke 18:18–27). Is this easy for you to do?

IT COST EVERYTHING

NO, MY LIFE & EVERYTHING IS GODS.

To be commissioned with compassion is an awesome responsibility. After all, are we very righteous and compassionate by nature? (see Rom. 3:10; Rom. 7:18; Mark 7:21.)

Describe your own sense of worthiness to be God's spokesperson and define what you base that worthiness on.

I AM WORTHY BECAUSE OF WHAT JESUS HAS DONE

If we're not very righteous or compassionate, how do we become that way? (See Psalm 51:10; John 7:38; John 15:4; 2 Corinthians 5:7.) *ALLOWING GOD TO CONTINUE TO WORK IN US*

Describe how the above scriptures have been confirmed or experienced in your life.

GOD PROMISES TO CONTINUE THE GOOD WORK WHICH HE HAS STARTED

Apparently, our dependence on the Lord is a significant key to being adequate to serve Him. It surely doesn't come from our own strength or design! Jesus wants us to follow Him closely. As we do, His character and His purposes will be fulfilled in and through us.

When Jesus said, "Follow Me!" to Peter, James, John, and Matthew, they immediately left everything and "followed" Him (Luke 5:10, 11, 27).

FAITH ALIVE

In your own words,

What do you think Jesus meant when He said "Follow Me"? Specifically, how is that to play out in our lives on a daily basis?

HE IS THE SHEPHERD & MODEL

What do you think it *doesn't* mean? (The answer is a bit tricky!)

WALKING BEHIND HIM

What has "following Jesus" meant to you? Has it been easy? Why or why not?

FOLLOWING HIS WILL FOR MY LIFE. NO, THERE IS SACRAFICE IN THE KINGDOM

KINGDOM EXTRA

Jesus is not vague or indecisive about anything, especially when it comes to people's accepting or rejecting the Good News! But why does Jesus sometimes speak in such intense terms, almost sounding angry, it seems? If God is love, why would He speak such sharp words?

His warnings are confrontive, but no less compassionate towards hearts hardened against Him. If a three-year-old child plays in the street after being repeatedly instructed not to do so, a parent's response will most likely be expressed with a fair degree of intensity; but that doesn't contradict love—it verifies it.

In the following references, Jesus addresses the issue of resistance toward the gospel. State in one or two sentences the underlying spiritual principle Jesus is teaching and what action should be taken in response to those principles.

Luke 8:4 – *PEOPLE WORE LOOKING FOR WHAT JESUS HAD FOR THEM. JESUS GAVE THEM THE ANSWER.*

Luke 9:5 – *WHEN PEOPLE REJECT WHAT GOD HAS, THE RESPOSIBILITY IS NOT OURS*

Luke 10:13–16 –

THE ACTIONS OF PEOPLE TOWARD YOU, ARE TOWARD GOD

Luke 11:29 – *THE PEOPLE LOOKED FOR MORE THAN WAS NEEDED*

Luke 12:9 – *DENYING GOD IS DENYING GOD BEFORE ALL OF CREATION*

✎ WORD WEALTH

Follow, *akoloutheo* (ak-ol-oo-*theh*-oh); *Strong's #190.* To accompany, to go along with, go the same way with, follow one who precedes. *A* means in union or likeness with, and *keluethos* is a road. *Akoloutheo* is being on the same roadway with someone. Since the word was used for soldiers, servants, and pupils, it can easily be transferred to the life of the Christian, a disciple of Christ. In seventy-eight occurrences in the Gospels, it is used seventy-seven times in connection with *following* Christ. Metaphorically, it is used for discipleship.[2]

❓ PROBING THE DEPTHS

What does the Scripture say in John 15:4–8 about union and likeness? *DON'T BE UNEQUALLY JOINED TOGETHER*

What can be expected when one abides "in the Vine"? (John 15:4–8) *FRUIT*

How does this relate to world evangelism? *WHEN WE ARE CONNECTED TO THE VINE OF GOD WE WILL SEE FRT*

Consistently abiding in Christ provides a way for Christ's life to flow into my life without interruption. His life flowing into me provides all the "divine DNA" I need to produce all that He is in daily living and empowers the possibility of His "likeness" being formed in me. That "likeness" can only happen when I abide in Him. Otherwise, I'm merely producing human sweat in trying to achieve the impossible. Jesus said, "Without Me you can do nothing." John 3:6 states:

> That which is born of the flesh is flesh, and that which is born of the Spirit is spirit.

 ## FAITH ALIVE

Is this command to "follow" and "abide" too much to ask? At what point do you, personally, begin holding back from following Jesus more closely? In what areas of your life do you most fear God "interfering" with your agenda?

Try this exercise: discuss your answers to the above questions with the Lord, out loud, in the car or in some secluded place. Explain to God why you feel (if, in fact, you do) something horrible will happen if you give Him complete control of your life. Maybe it's an unreasonable fear. Confess it to Him. If appropriate, laugh with God about how ridiculous it is. Confess any sin or unbelief, and ask Him to infuse you with new faith, strength, vision, hope—whatever it is you need to overcome such obstacles.

How might fulfilling the above exercise have an impact on personal evangelism?

 ## KINGDOM EXTRA

The people of Sri Lanka worship millions of gods. The spiritual darkness in that country is severe. How could the Gospel possibly reach people so blind and bound? Ask local pastor Leslie Keegel. Not long ago he met a man who typified the kind of bondage much of that society wrestles with. The man was a dwarf who was also mute and deaf and who suffered from sudden attacks of insanity. By anyone's standard, that is certainly suffocating darkness! Leslie prayed for this young Buddhist, and a number of demons were cast out of him. The man was immediately freed from insanity! His hearing was restored, and, within three days, he began speaking! And not only that, but hundreds of people with whom he'd lived witnessed his sudden growth from four feet tall to five-foot-five (the average height of a Sri Lankan male!)

Taking this formerly disabled young man under his wing, Leslie began training him in the ways of the Lord. As a result, he was filled with the Holy Spirit, began telling others of the miraculous power and love of Jesus Christ, and today, this beloved brother is a church pastor! "The darkness could not extinguish the light!"

Evangelism—it's not just words. It is Good News accompanied with love, power, and righteousness, resulting in changed lives which, in turn, continue to change lives! Could anything be more fulfilling than seeing people's lives turned around so they not only live for Jesus, but in time, bring others to Christ as well? The joy of being a part of such a wonderful witness, accompanied by God's power, transcends the thrill of other endeavors.

Now that you've studied this subject, without dwelling on the word too long, what picture comes to mind when you think about "evangelism" *now*.

1. *Spirit-Filled Life Bible* (Nashville: Thomas Nelson Publishers, 1991), 49, "Word Wealth: Gen. 29:32 son."

2. Ibid., 1601, "Word Wealth, John 13:36 follow."

Lesson 8/Evangelism According to John

The writer of the Gospel of John is often referred to as "Saint John the Evangelist." This is not because he was the only instrument of salvation or evangelism in the New Testament. It is more likely because he gives a very clear and easily understood gospel presentation.

Evangelistic ministries worldwide have traditionally given new or prospective converts a copy of the Gospel of John. John shows plainly who Jesus is and why He came to earth. John tells us plainly that Jesus came to earth to live that we might be saved from our sin and be reconciled to God. John tells the story of Jesus' life and how we may gain eternal life through His name.

THE GOSPEL'S PURPOSE

Near the end of his Gospel, John gives us his reason for writing this intimate account of the life of Christ. Read John 20:31 and write John's stated purpose below.

BELIEVE & HAVE LIFE

This statement makes it clear that the gospel is recorded with an evangelistic intent. John longed for the world to know Jesus as he did and to experience saving grace. If the church today could match the zeal and love of John the Apostle for his Savior, the world would indeed "know us by our love," and people would come much closer to what Jesus intended.

BEHIND THE SCENES

All the Gospels record how much John loved Jesus, and how devoted he was to the Lord's work. John was also privileged to be placed with Paul and Luke as one of the three most prolific writers of the New Testament. Name the other four New Testament books written by the Apostle John:

1. I John

2. II John

3. II John

4. Revalation

To be "born again" (John 3:3) refers to the specific life-changing experience of being made into a new person by the power of the Holy Spirit, who literally comes to live within one who becomes a believer in Jesus Christ. John's Gospel is the only place in the Bible where the "born again" requirement for salvation is so clearly established. Write out Jesus' words in John 3:3:

UNLESS ONE IS BORN AGAIN, HE CANNOT SEE THE KINGDOM OF GOD

"Again," He says in John 3:5:

MUST BE BORN AGAIN TO SEE THE KINGDOM OF HEAVEN

This same theme is substantiated in Paul's letter to the Romans:

> But you are not in the flesh but in the Spirit, if indeed the Spirit of God dwells in you. Now if anyone does not have the Spirit of Christ, he is not His. And if Christ is in you, the body is dead because of sin, but the Spirit is life because of righteousness. But if the Spirit of Him who raised Jesus from the dead dwells in you, He who raised Christ from the dead will also give life to your mortal bodies through His Spirit who dwells in you (Rom. 8:9–11).

There is no mincing of words here. The gospel message is unashamedly clear: Either you are born again by the Spirit of God or you do not belong to Christ and not in God's kingdom.

 KINGDOM EXTRA

Upon repentance, a new order of life opens to the believer in Jesus Christ. Jesus used the figure of "new birth" to dramatically indicate three things: 1) Without New Birth, there is no life and no relationship with God (14:6). 2) In New Birth, new perspective comes as we "see the kingdom of God" (3:3). God's Word becomes clear, and the Holy Spirit's works and wonders are believed and experienced—faith is alive. 3) Through New Birth we are introduced—literally we "enter" (v.5)—to a new realm, where God's new kingdom order can be realized (2 Cor. 5:17). New Birth is more than simply being "saved." It is a requalifying experience, opening up the possibilities of our whole being to the supernatural dimension of life and fitting us for a beginning in God's kingdom order.[1]

The gospel is further explained to be a *gift of love* from the Father who sent His only Son, Jesus, to be "lifted up" (crucified) for all of mankind's sin (John 3:14; 12:32). The most quoted verse in the Bible, John 3:16, says, "For God so loved the world that He gave His only begotten Son, that whoever believes in Him should not perish but have everlasting life."

This great demonstration of the love of God for those He created is the *crux* (Latin for cross) of the gospel. The gospel is indeed a gospel of love, yet it is seen as meaningless by a world that does not turn and embrace such love.

 FAITH ALIVE

Have you been born again? If not, and if you believe what you've just read, stop now and ask God to forgive you for your sins and send the Holy Spirit to live in you. He wants to do this more than you want Him to! He will do exactly what He says in the Bible. He will come and make you a "new creation" (1 Cor. 5:17). You will begin to see Him active in your life, blessing you, and helping you.

If you have done this, you have begun a personal relationship with Jesus Christ, the Son of God! Praise God for His wonderful salvation through Jesus Christ our Lord!

If you have done this, or if you've been born again for some time, write a short description of how it happened.

AT A VERY YOUNG AGE

I ASKED JESUS IN MY LIFE

JOHN'S WITNESS

Long before we get to Jesus' remarkable words of "good news" in John 3 ("gospel" means good news), the apostle tells us about the ministry of one of the greatest evangelists in history, John the Baptist. This unusual man was a powerful instrument of the Lord's. "There was a man sent from God, whose name was John. This man came for a witness, to bear witness of the Light, that all through him might believe. He was not that Light, but was sent to bear witness of that Light" (John 1:6–8).

WORD WEALTH

Bear witness, *martureo* (mar-too-*reh*-o). To be a witness, to bear witness, i.e., to affirm that one has seen or heard or experienced something, or that he knows it because of being taught by divine revelation or inspiration; to give (not to keep back) testimony; to utter honorable testimony, give a good report; conjure, implore. Clearly "bearing witness" is evangelization in its purest, most familiar—and most effective—form. John the Baptist was indeed sharing what he had been "taught by divine revelation." He was testifying to what God had sovereignly shown him. In addition to being anointed as a prophet of God, he was an evangelist in every respect. He brought the good news to those who would hear, and many responded in repentance and baptism for the forgiveness of sins.

John the Baptist made some important declarations about Jesus. Look these verses up and write them out after their references.

John 1:30

John 1:26, 27

John 1:29

John 1:34

Surely this is evangelism at its highest and best. How can we ever evangelize the lost and needy if we do not tell them who Jesus is and introduce them to Him?

In reaching to the lost, we may find ourselves having to establish who Jesus is from the Bible. People may ask honest questions about Jesus, and John has given us a definitive answer. Jesus is God.

The apostle begins his Gospel with strong and definitive theological statements. What is his main point about Jesus in each of the following verses?

John 1:1–2

v. 3

v. 4

v. 14

The first chapter of John's Gospel is one of the most decisive passages in Scripture declaring the essential truth that Jesus Christ is God. Cults have tried to change it or water it down because of its clarity and directness, but still it remains unquestionably clear.

FAITH ALIVE

Let's look more closely at Jesus' conversation with Nicodemus in John 3. There are ideas here that will profit us as we reach out to others with the gospel.

1) Nicodemus came to Jesus. He was hungry for the truth. Let us not push the salvation message "down the throats" of those who are not yet ready to hear it. Rather, we should pray for opportunities to "bear witness" and then wait on the Holy Spirit to lead us into the situations *He* directs. Then we will have His anointing and blessing on our witness.

2) Jesus was not distracted by flattery or misdirection. Nicodemus asked "all around" the topic he was really interested in. But Jesus discerned his soul's need and answered his *heart's* question, rather than that of his *words.* If we listen to the promptings of the Holy Spirit, and try to sense what folks are really saying, we can answer their questions.

3) Jesus quickly got the the point. He spoke directly and to the man's need. We may be inclined to "beat about the bush." Probably the Holy Spirit will lead us to a gentle approach, but we must remember that Jesus is the Bread of Life and not be hesitant to speak about His satisfying power with a hungry soul.

JOHN'S WRITINGS

John also documents some of the most profound words of Jesus, words which none of the synoptic writers recorded. Several of Jesus' statements in John's Gospel substantiate His divinity as no other words in the Bible. Look at the following verses and write the words of Jesus which best show that He is the Son of God and the Savior.

John 6:27–29

John 6:38–40

John 8:58

John 9:35–38

John 10:28–38

John 11:25–26

John 12:46–50

 WORD WEALTH

Savior, *soter* (so-*tare*); *Strong's #4990.* Compare "soteriology," the doctrine of salvation. From the same root as *sodzo,* "to save," and *soteria,* "salvation." The word designates a deliverer, preserver, savior, benefactor, rescuer. It is used to describe both God the Father and Jesus the Son.[2]

The verses above are fundamental in witnessing as to who our Lord is and what His purpose was in coming to earth. Our sharing with people should include: 1) telling them who Jesus is, 2) telling them He came to save us from the penalty of our sin, and 3) showing them that they can receive His great gift of salvation.

John also shows us what God the Father is like by showing us what Jesus His Son was like when He walked among men. We read Jesus' words to Philip, who asked Him, "Show us the Father." Jesus responded by saying, "If you have seen Me, you have seen the Father" (14:9). So, with Philip, when we look at what Jesus was like, how He treated people, and who He chose to spend His time with, we see an image of Father God. Jesus is Immanuel, "God with us," for us to see and experience what God our heavenly Father is like.

When we see Jesus healing the sick and casting out demons, or when we see Him reach out with compassion to the hurting or to comfort a helpless child, or when we see Him angry at sin yet speak forgiveness, we see what Father God is like.

God sent Jesus to be a revelation of Himself to us, to show us who He is and what He is like. He did this because He loves us. He loves us so much that He sent His beloved Son to suffer and die for our salvation. Surely God, our heavenly Father, is the greatest Evangelist of all!

JOHN'S PRIORITY

Another evangelism-related topic relates to the necessity of walking in the Spirit and thus being "linked" to Christ and the power we have in Him. In John 15:4–8, we read:

> Abide in Me, and I in you. As the branch cannot bear fruit of itself, unless it abides in the vine, neither can you, unless you abide in Me. I am the vine, you are the branches. He who abides in Me, and I in him, bears much fruit; for without Me you can do nothing. If anyone does not abide in Me, he is cast out as a branch and is withered; and they gather them and throw them into the fire, and they are burned. If you abide in Me, and My words abide in you, you will ask what you desire, and it shall be done for you. By this My Father is glorified, that you bear much fruit; so you will be My disciples.

The tendency here is to identify the "fruit" in this passage with converts for the kingdom of God. But the real fruit is a "connected" life, the life of one who is "abiding in the Vine." And of course, if we abide in Christ, we will become more like Him and radiate more of His love to others.

God's love always has been the major attraction to Jesus. It is what drew men to Him when He walked the earth 2000 years ago. When people saw how He loved, they could not resist coming to Him and receiving what He had to offer. And the things He offered them were from His vast storehouse of love. The people who came to Him inevitably received gifts of healing, deliverance, and salvation. If we become more like Christ, we will *naturally* bring others into His presence and see them healed, delivered, and saved.

The word "abide" means "to live in" or "to remain in." So, one might ask, how do we live or remain "connected" to Jesus, the Source of love and power? According to John 15:1–17, what is Jesus' answer to this question?

GOD IS THE VINE / WE ARE THE BRANCHES

Though Jesus calls us to obedience, it may seem impossible because we are still clay vessels and sinful. But Jesus made obedience easier than it would seem when He summed the commandments up with, "Love God and one another." When Jesus said this, He was not asking us to *feel* like loving, but to love.

PROBING THE DEPTHS

The Bible's definition of love is not the same as the world's. Yet it is the world's description of love that people see most. It has to do primarily with sexual attraction and the acting out of immorality. As far as one can tell, that is all there is to love.

Love in the Bible is pictured as a commitment; a decision one makes to be committed to another person, whether in marriage or in friendship. Love is the result of one person *deciding* to love another by his or her *actions.* When a man washes the dishes for his wife, he is loving her. When a man mows his neighbor's lawn when he is on vacation, he is loving his neighbor. The result of this love can be warm, affectionate feelings for one another, but the feelings *follow* the act of love.

Jesus calls us to this kind of love. He even said that when we keep His commands, we are, in fact, loving Him!

In his first epistle, John said some of the same things that we have seen in his Gospel. What are three themes you see in I John 2:6–10 that are in common with the verses we have been discussing?

GRACE RELEASED

Jesus is looking for people who will abide in His presence, be obedient to His Word, and love one another. Obeying His commands and loving each other are one and the same thing; if we love, we are being obedient. And if we are obedient, we are loving Him. People who love are the ones the Lord uses to accomplish His evangelistic purposes in the earth. He wants to release gifts of grace through each and every one of His disciples, so the world will see our love—for each other and for them—and come to Him. John makes this clear throughout his gospel, "By this all will know that you are My disciples, if you have love for one another" (John 13:35). And he continues in his epistles to preach this same message he learned from Jesus, "For this is the message that you heard from the beginning, that we should love one another" (1 John 3:11).

 PROBING THE DEPTHS

For John, Jesus' humanity meant essentially a twofold mission: 1) As the "Lamb of God" (1:29), He procured the redemption of mankind; 2) Through His life and ministry He revealed the Father. Christ consistently pointed beyond Himself to the Father who had sent Him and whom He sought to glorify. In fact, the very miracles Jesus performed, which John characterized as "signs," bore testimony to the divine mission of the Son of God. As the Son glorified the Father in ministry and passion, so the Father glorified the Son. But, as John shows, the Son's glorification came at the Crucifixion (12:32, 33), not only in the postresurrection exaltation. By believing that Jesus is the Christ, the readers of John's gospel become participants in the life Jesus brought out of death (20:31).[3]

If Jesus dwells in us as born again believers, then His works in and through us will also testify of Him to the world. If we walk in the power of the Spirit and allow Him to do the works He desires to do, these works will testify of His grace, love, and power to the world. It is for this purpose we are commissioned by Christ and empowered by His Spirit:

> So Jesus said to them again, "Peace to you! As the Father has sent Me, I also send you" (John 20:21).
> But you shall receive power when the Holy Spirit has come upon you; and you shall be witnesses to Me in Jerusalem, and in all Judea and Samaria, and to the end of the earth (Acts 1:8).

The disciples had had three and a half years of face-to-face following, watching, listening, learning, and doing in order to be *sent in like manner*. Christians had been discipled; now they were being sent into a mission field to be witnesses and to make more disciples.

WORD WEALTH

Sent, *apostello* (ap-os-*tel*-low); *Strong's #649*. To commission, set apart for a special service, send a message by someone, send out with a mission to fulfill, equip and dispatch one with the full backing and authority of the sender.[4]

Jesus' words in John 20:21 (above) were a summons for the disciples to bring their personal agendas into alignment with God's purposes. Jesus said, "As the Father has sent Me, I also send you." The message could be paraphrased: "As I modeled obedience to the Father, always doing what He said, so you do that now in your going forth, rendering obedience to Me."

KINGDOM EXTRA

John's Gospel presents the deity of Jesus—the Son of God. As God He has created all things (1:1–3), and as God He has come to redeem all—to bring the fullness of forgiveness. This aspect of His mission is conveyed to His disciples as their commission as well: Go with forgiveness. It is stated here as both a mandate and a mission: 1) "I also send you." Precisely as the Father sent the Son to bring salvation as an availability to every human being (3:16), so we are sent to insure that availability is understood by everyone. 2) "If you forgive" indicates the conditional nature of His provision. It cannot be responded to unless it is delivered. There is no escape from the awesome nature of His terminology here. We are not only sent with the substance of the message—salvation; we are sent to bring the spirit of its truth—forgiveness. Only the breath of His Spirit, which He breathed upon those who first heard these words, can enable us to go obediently and to reach lovingly. The message (salvation) and its meaning (forgiveness) are ours to deliver, and we need to receive the Holy Spirit to do both.[5]

1. *Spirit-Filled Life Bible* (Nashville: Thomas Nelson Publishers, 1991), 1577, "Kingdom Dynamics, John 3:1–5, New Birth."

2. Ibid., 1581, "Word Wealth, John 4:42 Savior."

3. Ibid., 1572, "Christ Revealed."

4. Ibid., 1614, "Word Wealth, John 20:21 sent."

5. Ibid., 1614, "Kingdom Dynamics, John 20:21–23, Commissioned with a Mandate and a Message."

Lesson 9/*Evangelism without Fear*

Fear takes many forms and has many sources. Earthquakes, fires, floods, tornadoes, cancer, prolonged illness, and people can be the cause of debilitating fear in our lives. However, with God's help, guidance, and intervention, we try to face our fears and become stronger in our Christian walk as a result.

Then one Sunday the pastor preaches about witnessing and evangelism, and we become fearful again. Why is there fear in many hearts when it comes to witnessing and evangelism? How does it come? What do we do about it?

 PROBING THE DEPTHS

How is the word "fear" used in the following verses.

Exodus 15:16

Exodus 20:20

Proverbs 29:25

Isaiah 8:13

Hosea 3:5

Matthew 10:26–28

Philippians 1:14

Hebrews 11:27

Hebrews 13:6

WORD WEALTH

Fear, *morah* (moh-*rah*); *Strong's #4172:* Fear, reverence, terror, awe; an object of fear, respect, or reverence. *Morah* is derived from *yare',* "to be afraid of, to fear, to reverence." *Morah* occurs a dozen times in the Old Testament, beginning with Genesis 9:2, which speaks of the fear and dread Noah's descendants would inspire in all animals after the Flood. The Lord also inspires fear, as in Psalm 76:11. In the present reference, Isaiah (8:13) is admonished never to fear human threats, but to let God alone be the object of his reverential fear.[1]

LEARNING FROM THE PAST

We're not the only ones who have feared sharing God with others. There are examples of fearful evangelists in both the Old and New Testaments. A review of some of their stories will help us see how fear influenced their lives and what response God made to free them so they could be used in His purposes.

God had spared Moses at birth and arranged for him to be educated in the finest schools of Egypt. Through this, Moses became a leader to serve a larger plan than he could know or guess.

But Moses spent forty years thinking he was somebody. After another forty years out in the desert exiled from Egypt, he realized he was really a nobody. His last forty years were spent finding out what God can do with a nobody.

Where would you place yourself in those three areas and why?

THE LAST 40 YRS, GOD HAS BROUGHT ME TO BEING AVAILABLE

How do you deal with negativism?

CUT IT OUT

How does your life parallel that of Moses?

I BELIEVE EVERYONE HAS SOME LARITIES

Exodus 3—4 is the setting where Moses discovered that God uses nobodies. Moses had resigned himself to be a shepherd for the remainder of his years, but God's call was true.

Are you a person ready to allow God to form and shape you into a nobody He can use?

HERE I AM LORD, USE ME

 PROBING THE DEPTHS

Let's examine how God changes someone into a shepherd. Often we use excuses for not answering the call of God on our lives. Read Exodus 3:1–8, and then answer the second and third columns below by looking up the first.

Reference	Moses' Response	God's Promise
3:9–12		
3:13–25		
4:1–9		
4:10–12		
4:13–17		

LEARNING EVANGELISM FROM AN EIGHTY-YEAR-OLD

We usually see Moses as a great man of God, which he was. However, becoming a man who could evangelize both Egypt and Israel necessitated overcoming many fears.

- *Fear of insignificance.* No one knows me. I'm too young or inexperienced. (1 Tim. 4:11–12)

- *Fear of being alone.* Do I have to do this alone? Are you, God, going to be there? (John 14:16–18). Hudson Taylor said, "God's work done in God's way will not lack God's support."
- *Fear of failure.* What if you can't or don't deliver your people? I'll look like a fool. (Mark 16:15–20, especially v. 20)
- *Fear of talking.* I have a speech problem. I don't talk very well. (See Ex. 12 and Jer. 1:6–10)
- *Fear of trying.* Send someone else—the pastor, elder, deacon, evangelist—not me. (John 21:15–17)

FAITH ALIVE

In what ways do you identify with the above fears?

IN SOME WAYS ALL

What could be the basis of your fears?

SELF / LIES OF THE ENEMY

How can you change with the Holy Spirit's help?

ALLOW THE HS TO WORK IN ME

Moses went back to Egypt, obeyed God, and God never let him down. Fear can keep us from proclaiming God's saving Word to people. When we give in to fear, we can still be saved, but never know what it's like to walk in the blessing of God.

JONAH: A PREJUDICED MAN

The book of Jonah contains some tremendous lessons about the battle between man's flesh and his spirit. Jonah was a man from Israel called by God to preach to the Assyrians in Nineveh. Rather than respond to the call to go, Jonah thought he could escape by traveling in the opposite direction.

⧉ BEHIND THE SCENES

The prophet Jonah visited Nineveh during the glorious days of the Assyrian empire. From about 885 to 625 B.C., the Assyrians dominated the ancient world. Numerous passages in the Old Testament report advances of Assyrian military forces against the neighboring kingdoms of Judah and Israel during these years. As early as 841 B.C., Jehu, king of Israel, was forced to pay tribute to the dominating Assyrian ruler, Shalmaneser III. This kind of harassment continued for over a century until Israel finally fell to Assyrian forces about 722 B.C. No wonder Jonah was reluctant to go to Nineveh; God had called him to visit the very heartland of enemy territory and to give the hated Assyrians a chance to repent! It was a radical order that would have taxed the obedience of any prophet. Jonah's grudging attitude should not blind us to the fact that he did carry out God's command.[2]

FAITH ALIVE

Take several minutes to read the short book of Jonah. Afterward, answer the following questions.

What was the basis of Jonah's fears?

How did God respond to the actions of a pagan city and why?

What have you learned about yourself from Jonah?

Do you fear responding to God's call?

Are you afraid God will show mercy to people you judge are undeserving?

Whose Spirit (spirit) is directing your life?

God called Jonah to evangelize, but his prejudice prevented it until God demonstrated His power. God is looking for willing, obedient people to do His work. Are you willing? How far can He send you? Only as we allow God to mold us like Moses and break us like Jonah will we be ready to evangelize under the power of the Holy Spirit.

FEARFUL PEOPLE IN THE NEW TESTAMENT

Moses tried to convince God that He had made a mistake in selecting him to be His mouthpiece. Jonah feared that God would show mercy to Nineveh. These are Old Testament examples. Are there examples of fear in witnessing in the New Testament, especially after the empowerment of the Holy Spirit on the Day of Pentecost? Doesn't God get rid of all fear when we are full of His Spirit?

Experience teaches that we do at times fear. Perhaps you experienced a time when you met someone and automatically felt fear because of what you may have heard about that individual. If so, you are in good company with Ananias in Acts 9. God told him to go pray for a new convert, Saul (Paul). He was reluctant to go due to what he had heard about Saul. But with God's loving encouragement, Ananias eventually went to witness to Saul.

PROBING THE DEPTHS

What can you find out about Ananias from Acts 9:10–19? Feel free to use the marginal references and footnotes from your study Bible. You may want to use the following questions and scriptures as starters. Review Acts 9:10–17 and 22:12–16. What kind of man was Ananias that God would call him to evangelize?

What compelled him to go to Saul?

How had God prepare the way for Ananias to see Saul?

The real question here is: how did Ananias overcome his fear?

Describe a time in your life where you were fearful to talk to someone based on what you had heard about the person.

How did you deal with that fear?

What passages in the Bible could have helped you overcome?

Ananias will share with Paul in heavenly rewards due to his decision to obey. As with Ananias, the Holy Spirit is prepared to help you overcome. Are you ready? Then let's learn how to overcome fear.

CHALLENGING FEAR

In a Spirit-filled walk, when fear arises it must be challenged (2 Tim. 1:7; 1 John 4:18). Unchallenged, fear will bring degrees of paralysis, which will affect our ability to be witnesses.

There are two men in the midst of evangelistic endeavors who were challenged about their fears. Fill in the chart on the next page by looking up the references and answering the questions.

Galatians 2:11–21

Who was the man?

Who did he challenge?

Why did he challenge them?

How did they change?

Acts 12:25, 15:36–41; 2 Timothy 4:11

Who was the man?

Who did he challenge?

Why did he challenge them?

How did they change?

✎ WORD WEALTH

Hypocrite, hupokrisis (*hoop*-ok-ree-sis); *Strong's #5272.* Literally, "a reply." The word came to denote a theatrical performer who spoke in dialogue. Then it was used of playacting, role-playing, pretending; hence, acting insincerely, hypocrisy.[3]

THE EARLY CHRISTIANS SPOKE BOLDLY

The early church boldly proclaimed the Word of God. Look up the following verses and make notes about boldness as the Holy Spirit impresses you.

Acts   2:14

3:11–12

4:8

4:13

4:29–33

7:54–56

9:20–22, 26–30

13:46

14:3

14:21–22

CONCLUSIONS

Romans 1:16–17 sets forth Paul's conclusion on the matter: he was not ashamed of the gospel. Could it be that lurking beneath our fear is shame?

If we are unashamed, we'll proclaim the gospel.

Fear like this is a spiritual problem, and requires a spiritual answer. The answer is found in believing the Word of God. God's Word is true and lasts forever. You *can* be a witness for Christ.

By daily acting on God's Word, fear can be overcome. Study these last four scriptures about overcoming fear in spreading the gospel, and write out your insights.

Eph. 6:11–13

2 Tim. 1:7

1 John 4:18

Rev. 12:11

Revelation 12:11 prophesies that end-time believers will overcome the enemy "by appropriating the victory of the finished work of Christ, by the public confession of their faith and patient endurance, even in the face of martyrdom" (Rev. 13:10). The church's constant posture under the authority of the Cross's victory by the blood of the lamb and steadfastness to the promise and authority of God's Word—the word of their testimony—is the key to their overcoming.[4]

 KINGDOM EXTRA

In Isaiah 40:8–11, the prophet declares the eternal reminder: "The word of our God stands forever," and then anticipates the spread of that word. The world needs a sound foundation upon which to build life, just as surely as it needs a sure salvation to redeem it. "Zion"—the people of God—have that word and are privileged to bring these "good tidings"—the pleasant, happy, and wholesome news of life now and hope forever. Thus 1) "Lift up your voice" (v. 9). The message is to proclaim good tidings, for nothing will happen until that declaration is made. 2) "Be not afraid" (v. 9); for God will manifest Himself as the proclaimer says, "Behold your God!" (v. 9). 3) Our message of One who has strength to rule, "a strong *hand,*" and a reward to give, (*"is* with Him," v. 10) will be confirmed. Answering our call to spread "good tidings," we are wise to be fearlessly obedient, believing God to confirm His word (Mark 16:20). Jesus tells of the servant who buried his talent, saying, "I was afraid!" Let God's perfect love and powerful promise cast out fears, and speak "Behold," to those He allows us to address with His Good News. He will confirm His word with proving power.[5]

God has called us to evangelize. After studying this chapter, what changes will occur in your life?

1. *Spirit-Filled Life Bible* (Nashville: Thomas Nelson Publishers, 1991), 973, "Word Wealth, Is. 8:13 fear."
2. *Nelson Illustrated Bible Dictionary* (Nashville: Thomas Nelson, Publishers, 1986), 590 "Jonah."
3. *Spirit-Filled Life Bible,* 1775, "Word Wealth, Gal. 2:13 hypocrite."
4. Ibid., 1977, study note on Rev. 12:11.
5. Ibid., 1012, "Kingdom Dynamics, Is. 40:8–11, Spread the Good Tidings—Fearlessly."

Lesson 10/ Taking the Gospel Everywhere

Before His crucifixion, Jesus told his disciples about the signs of the times which would occur near the end of this age. He presented a picture of the world's conditions before His return. Among those predicted events was His statement in Matthew 24:14, "And this gospel of the kingdom will be preached in all the world as a witness to all nations, and then the end will come."

This prophecy has become both an evangelistic goal and a hallmark of hope for disciples ever since. The goal has compelled believers to heroic steps in world evangelization. And the unfinished task has given the hope that there is yet time to reach both loved ones and lost tribes with the gospel "while it is day; the night is coming when no one can work" (John 9:4).

Having studied the earlier lessons in this guide, how would you now define the "gospel of the kingdom" to which Jesus referred in Matthew 24:14?

What aspects of "the kingdom" are new to you?

With all the "gospel surplus" in Christianized nations, why has the church not been successful in reaching "all the nations" with the gospel?

How has the "the gospel of the kingdom . . . preached in all the world" affected the kingdom of darkness, which has captivated and manipulated millions? (See Matt. 11:12; 2 Cor. 10:3–5; Eph. 6:11, 12.)

🗡 **WORD WEALTH**

Gospel, *euangelion* (yoo-ang-*ghel*-ee-on); *Strong's #2098*. Compare "evangel," "evangelize," "evangelistic." In ancient Greece *euangelion* designated the reward given for bringing good news. Later it came to mean the good news itself. In the New Testament the word includes both the promise of salvation and its fulfillment by the life, death, resurrection, and ascension of Jesus Christ. *Euangelion* also designates the written narratives of Matthew, Mark, Luke, and John.[1]

Review the references to the "Great Commission" (Matt. 28:18–20; Mark 16:15–18; Luke 24:46–49) and list any specific content which is to be preached in this redemptive kingdom message.

PUTTING THINGS IN PERSPECTIVE

Matthew 24:1, we read that Jesus and His disciples had just left the temple area in Jerusalem. The disciples beheld its structures with awe and admiration and called Jesus' attention to them. However, in the eyes of the Spirit, Jesus saw the temple in total ruin.

How did He describe what He saw to his disciples? (v. 2)

Later, as they sat with Him on the Mount of Olives (v. 3), still bewildered by His words, they asked Him more. They had thought that He would fulfill their immediate aspiration for an Israel liberated from Roman tyranny. They saw themselves living in freedom and triumph, with Jesus reigning over the House of David as their earthly, politically-crowned king. Now reality is dawning, and they are asking Him more questions.

What are the three questions they ask? (v. 3)

1)

2)

3)

In Matthew 24 and 25, Jesus answers the questions. Search these chapters for Jesus' answers and record the references and a brief summary statement below.

1st question:

2nd question:

3rd question:

WORD WEALTH

Signs, *semeion* (say-*mi*-on); *Strong's #4592.* Compare "semiology," "semiotic," "semaphore." A sign, mark, token. The word is used to distinguish between persons or objects (Matt. 26:48; Luke 2:12); to denote a warning or admonition (Matt. 12:39; 16:4); as an omen portending future events (Mark 13:4; Luke 21:7); to describe miracles and wonders, whether indicating divine authority (Matt. 12:38, 39; Mark 8:11, 12) or ascribed to false teachers and demons (Matt. 24:24; Rev. 16:14).[2]

Coming, *parousia* (par-oo-*see*-ah); *Strong's #3952.* The technical term signifying the second advent of Jesus was never used to describe His first coming. *Parousia* originally was the official term for a visit by a person of high rank, especially a king. It was an arrival that included a permanent presence from that point forward. The glorified Messiah's arrival will be followed by a permanent residence with His glorified people.[3]

Most scholars believe that biblical prophecy is often capable of both a near and a distant or future fulfillment. In answering the first question, you will probably find that Jesus uses the tragic events surrounding the destruction of Jerusalem as a picture of things to come, whose near fulfillment would have been about A.D. 70 and whose distant fulfillment is projected as preceding His own return.[4]

THE FOCUS IS JESUS

Jesus' primary concern is for His disciples, so He responds to their most immediate need. In Matthew 24:4 and 5, what is His first concern?

Yes, He is concerned that they be anchored in truth and following God's authentic Son, not a false christ. In other words, let us not get so caught up in last day events that we forget the King and eternal Son, who deserves our primary attention. His name is to be heralded to the world, to all peoples and all nations.

Jesus does not want His disciples to fall prey to the deceiver. What does Jesus say about Satan? How will Satan carry out his deception? Summarize verses 4, 5, 11, and 23–25 below.

The apostles of the early church expressed the same concern. Summarize their thoughts in the following scriptures in the context of today's world.

Colossians 2:8

Colossians 2:18–19

1 John 2:18, 22

TROUBLE EVERYWHERE

In Matthew 24:6–13, Jesus deals with the gloominess of a godless world rushing to its last hurrah at the "end of the ages." Write down what strikes you most as you read these verses.

Compare these predictions with Revelation 6:3–8.

Jesus explains what must come to pass as we persevere in the commission's completion, taking the gospel around the world. From Matthew 24:5–8, make a verse-by-verse list of the dreadful times and circumstances Jesus described, which His disciples may face wherever they live and witness throughout these last days.

Matt. 24:5

v. 6

v. 7

v. 8

We see that "wars and rumors of wars" exist all around us now. Matthew 24:6 says, "See that you are not troubled." What do you believe is meant by this admonition?

How we can handle these times and not be "troubled?"

⚔ WORD WEALTH

Age, *aion* (ahee-*ohn*); *Strong's #165.* Denotes an indefinitely long period, with emphasis on the characteristics of the period rather than on its duration. In idiomatic usage it designates "forever" or "forever and ever" (Rom. 16:27; Eph. 3:21). The word is also used as a designation for the present age (Matt. 12:32; 13:22; 1 Tim. 6:17) and for the time after Christ's Second Coming (Mark 10:30; Luke 20:35).[5]

The deceptiveness of false messiahs and prophets, wars and rumors of wars, kingdoms rising against kingdoms, and natural disasters such as famines, pestilences, and earthquakes will precede His coming. The sorrow that results, like unrelenting waves crashing upon the beach, will erode everything not built upon the Rock (Matt. 24:6–8). Hopefully, the sorrow will be godly sorrow that leads to repentance, not the sorrow that comes of material loss and human poverty.

The sorrow that will come *can* be handled by believers as they embrace Jesus, the all-compassionate One. Isaiah 53:3 and 4 and

Hebrews 4:14–16 explain what kind of Man He is. Write your perception of Him below.

PROBING THE DEPTHS

The Bible reveals how godly character develops in those who become filled with God's love, His life, and compassion for the people of our world. Note the enrichment that is present in the following passages.

Genesis 18:23–33

Proverbs 29:18

Revelation 5:10; 8:3, 4

THE PROGRESS OF TIME, THE INCREASE OF PRESSURE

Many intercessors become directly involved in the answer to their prayers. The gospel can, when brought in wisdom and timeliness, turn the tide and defuse the most volatile of situations, even at the height of a battle or in the most heated conflict.

How does Revelation 12:11 describe the dedication of end-time disciples?

Do you think believers in America will have to face martyrdom? (See Revelation 13:10.)

In Matthew 24:8–12, one sees the increase of persecution, which will either bring believers closer to the Lord or wash them away. But Jesus is able to keep that which is committed unto Him (2 Tim. 1:12). From Matthew 24, list what believers who are committed to the end are going to face?

Matt. 24:9

v. 10

v. 11

v. 12

Jesus provided hope and a promise when He said, "he who endures to the end shall be saved" (Matt. 24:13). How do New Testament writers say we should conduct ourselves in the following verses?

Phil. 1:27–30

Heb. 10:38–39

WORD WEALTH

Endures, *hupomeno* (hoop-ahm-*en*-oh); *Strong's #5278.* To hold one's ground in conflict, bear up against adversity, hold out under stress, stand firm, persevere under pressure, wait calmly and courageously. It is not passive resignation to fate and

mere patience, but the active, energetic resistance to defeat that
allows calm and brave endurance.[6]

In the midst of calamity, the church in triumph breaks
through (Rev. 10:11; 14:6) to free Satan's powerless captives by
declaring the Name of One who frees and brings life. Paul says
that in order to be able to endure, we must put on the Lord Jesus
Christ (Rom. 13:12, 14). He is all we need (1 Cor. 1:29–31).
Putting on Jesus is, in part, like putting on all the armor described
in Ephesians 6:14–16. Below, list each piece of the armor, and
how Jesus becomes all we need.

Those who walk in the Spirit have God's power and presence
to accomplish His purposes. The natural, carnal mind always
fumbles and fails in the heat of its battles (Romans 8:1–11; 1 Pet.
5:8). But Jesus is our truth and our "breastplate of righteousness."
He shods our feet with His gospel, which we take into the world.
Having received Jesus as the shield of our faith and the helmet of
our salvation, together with the sword of His Spirit in our hand
and in our mouth, we submit all to be done in Christ Jesus by the
Spirit through prayer warfare. The Spirit of victory will always
attend our way.

What is the warrior's first stance of defense? Review the
following Scriptures, and then describe the stance. (Acts 13:2–3;
16:9; 18:9–10; Rom. 1:13–17; 13:12, 14; 2 Cor. 4:6; 6:7; 10:3–8;
1 Thes. 5:8–9)

What is his second stance? Acts 9:20–25 says Paul entered the
Jewish synagogue, which was where he often got caught in chaotic
resistance and cross fire. Can you think of an instance in which
either you or someone you know has met this type of situation?
Describe it here.

PROBING THE DEPTHS

The idea in Matthew 11:12 is that the kingdom of heaven, which Jesus set up as a powerful movement or reign among men (suffers violence), and requires of them an equally strong and radical reaction. The violent then who take it by force are people of keen enthusiasm and commitment and are willing to respond to and propagate with radical abandonment the message and dynamic of God's reign (see Luke 16:16).[7]

This all points to present victories over the powers of darkness, as well as the ultimate destruction of Satan's kingdom at Jesus' Second Coming.

In conjunction with Matthew 24:13, many have given, and will give, their all. They will, in varying measure, suffer gladly and greatly (Matt. 10:35–39; Mark 10:28–30; Rom. 8:18; Col. 1:24, Phil. 1:20–21; 3:7–14.

 PROBING THE DEPTHS

In John 16:33, Jesus talks about good cheer. However, this verse is only a part of Jesus' larger teaching in John 13:21—17:26. He knows His disciples will be facing gravely disturbing times of tribulation. The Greek definition of tribulation adds tension to His words.

 WORD WEALTH

Tribulation, *thlipsis* (*thlip*-sis); *Strong's #2347.* Pressure, oppression, stress, anguish, tribulation, adversity, affliction, crushing, squashing, squeezing, distress. Imagine placing your hand on a stack of loose items and manually compressing them. That is *thlipsis,* putting a lot of pressure on that which is free and unfettered. *Thlipsis* is like spiritual bench-pressing. The word is used of crushing grapes or olives in a press.[8]

ON MAN'S TERMS, OR GOD'S?

All that was happening in the world then and all that is coming to pass today is the result of mankind's trying to make life happen on their own terms. God's terms or ways are not man's, for God's ways are higher. That is why possessing cheerfulness amid tribulation is possible only in following Jesus' order of trust in times of chaos. Being an overcomer is possible.

Lyle Storey writes, "As Jesus sketches the prevailing conditions of their present age down to the very end and states their continuing task, He says that in the midst of the difficulties, the Lord's followers are to persevere in spreading the Gospel."

CONCLUSION

The church of Jesus Christ must pray. A Holy Spirit vision needs to be ignited. Globally minded, missiological strategists must come together. People called of God to go must prepare and present themselves. Preparations to send and support need to be set in order. The Holy Spirit, of necessity, will call the church to fasting and prayer, and call some to go forth in service to the nations.

 FAITH ALIVE

Taking the gospel to the streets, whether at home or abroad, is a desire of most Christians. And probably all Christians desire to pray for the lost. So all of us are involved at some level. Whether you want to pray or to go, below are some ideas that may help you fulfill your desire. Make a note to yourself in the areas that will be applicable for you.

- Follow international news and ask the Lord to give you prayer burdens for certain stories or hotspots. Write those here.

- Follow local or national news for burdens to pray for individuals who you determine really need Jesus.

- Assess your life honestly and list below the things that tend to get in the way of your doing evangelism.

- On the positive side, list the provisions and characteristics God has given you for doing evangelism.

- Set a practical goal. Be realistic. Write down one or two ways during the next six months to a year that you can get involved evangelistically. Ideas: one-on-one with a neighbor, working in your church's evangelistic activities, doing a short-term missions outreach. Take some time, prayerfully, with a friend or a spouse to decide, and make a commitment here, on paper, that you will be faithful to.

1. *Spirit-Filled Life Bible* (Nashville: Thomas Nelson Publishers, 1991), 1468, "Word Wealth, Mark 1:1 gospel."
2. Ibid., 1984, "Word Wealth: Rev. 16:14 signs."
3. Ibid., 1744, "Word Wealth: 1 Cor. 15:23 coming."
4. Ibid., 1451, study note on Matt. 24:1–51.
5. Ibid., 1464, "Word Wealth: Matt. 28:20 age."
6. Ibid., 1451, "Word Wealth: Matt. 24:13 endures."
7. Ibid., 1424, study note on Matt. 11:12.
8. Ibid., 1607, "Word Wealth: John 16:33 tribulation."

Lesson 11/ *Supernaturally Equipped*

Three divine provisions enabled the early church to fulfill its work and mission: 1) Our Lord's disciples were supernaturally equipped with power for service by the baptism of the Holy Spirit (Acts 1:8); 2) They were prompted to proclaim faithfully and forcefully the Word of God (Acts 8:4); 3) Gifted church leaders cultivated individual believers and oversaw corporate ministries (Eph. 4:11–16), which resulted in the body's natural expansion (numerical growth) and edification (spiritual growth).

The church has always suffered when these essential elements were neglected. To any extent that they are neglected, the spread of the Good News is hindered.

Which of these three areas is the primary focus in your church fellowship?

Which, if any, is currently neglected in your fellowship?

EQUIPPED WITH POWER TO SERVE

Traditionally we understand that the church began on the day of Pentecost. This was one of three times each year when the Jews were required by the Law to go to Jerusalem to celebrate a feast. What were the other two occasions? (See Deut. 16:16; Lev. 23:15–16.)

After His resurrection, until he was "taken up . . . into heaven," what was the theme of Jesus' teaching? (See Acts 1:3.)

What related question did the disciples ask in verse 6?

God's kingdom and its power must be received by whose assistance and authority? (See Acts 1:8.)

This power and authority is available for what times? (Acts 2:38–39.)

"Church" is frequently not used in its New Testament sense today. Today we may speak of the church as a:
  building—"Our church is located at 7th Avenue and 23rd Street."
  denomination—"Our church has more members in foreign countries than here at home"; or
  social institution—"The church opposes pornography and abortion."
  The church in the New Testament stood for the people of God. It is not a building we inhabit. It is a building that is made up of believers as "living stones." The walls do not enclose the faithful; rather, the faithful are the walls. We are members of a body, belonging to each other, not members of a building.

 PROBING THE DEPTHS

We hear much in this scientific age of various organ transplants—kidneys, hearts, and other organs. At the moment of salvation God performs a supernatural operation by which we are "delivered . . . from the power of darkness and conveyed . . . into the kingdom of the Son of His love" (Col. 1:13). He then assigns us the role of a distinct part in His body and grafts us into that body. It's *His* body. He is the head and He decides how its parts are to serve His purposes and plans.

Man's efforts at transplants have not been too successful. At best they just prolong life a few years. But the body God is putting together to glorify Himself will live forever. He carefully equips and empowers each part with all that is needed to contribute to a dynamic eternal body that He has planned!

The apostle Paul seemed to see himself as a military commander, and throughout his writings he challenged us to realize we are in a war with the devil. Much of his teaching was centered on a spiritual form of military training.

One such area of training is found in Ephesians 6. Here, and elsewhere, the apostle instructs about 1) the enemies we face, 2) the armor we have been given, 3) the weapons and resources we have, and 4) our victorious response.

What four kinds of spiritual rebels are mentioned in Ephesians 6:11 and 12?

1.

2.

3.

4.

What are we to stand against?

 PROBING THE DEPTHS

The schemes and strategies of Satan can be better understood when you consider some of the names the Bible uses for this arch enemy. Look up the following passages to determine "the top ten New Testament names of our evil enemy."

Matt. 4:3	Matt. 12:26
Matt. 13:19	John 8:44a
John 8:44b	John 14:30
2 Cor.4:4	Eph. 2:1–2
Heb. 2:14	1 Pet. 5:8

Identify the parts of our spiritual armor from Ephesians 6:14–16, and match them with the explanatory statements below:
- Unswerving confidence in the Word
- Assurance of our salvation
- Moral integrity
- Enabling us to stand firm and to move quickly
- Sincerity, truthful objectivity as to our spiritual standing and state

👑 KINGDOM EXTRA

According to the New Testament writers—all of whom mention Satan and wicked spirits—demons are our invisible enemies. They are real, not imagined. They have personalities, and they can think and talk. They are invisible spirit beings who desire to inhabit bodies of human beings and animals, or even inanimate objects associated with evil or idolatry.

Biblical evidence supports the understanding that demons are fallen angels. When Lucifer, one of the heavenly archangels, rebelled against God in his prideful desire to be like the Most High God, he carried with him an army of followers. We've been in a spiritual warfare ever since.

Related to our defensive armor are our offensive weapons and spiritual resources. What is the sword of the Spirit? (Eph. 6:17)

When Christ was tempted, he quoted Scripture. What was the result? (Matt. 4:11)

What does James tell us to do to be able to see the Devil flee from us? (James 4:7)

To be fully equipped for spiritual warfare we must also learn to utilize another key resource: prayer (Eph. 4:18). We have great authority in prayer, based on our identification with Christ's death and resurrection (Rom. 6). Our authority in Christ allows us to speak against Satan and evil spirits in prayer. Jesus said we have authority to bind and loose (Matt. 18:18).

How did Paul indicate we are to "pray at all times"? (Eph. 6:18)

What spiritual value is there in "praying in the Holy Spirit"? (Jude 20)

What is a practical reason for Spirit-directed prayer? (Rom. 8:26–27)

If we are to spread the Good News effectively, we must be supernaturally equipped with power for service and spiritual warfare by the Holy Spirit. Only then we can expectantly pray, "Thy Kingdom come. Thy will be done on earth, as it is in heaven."

EQUIPPED WITH POWER TO PROCLAIM

Like the early apostles, the prophet Isaiah's passion was to declare the Word of God. Out of God's touch on his life, not born from personal emotion, Isaiah lifted his voice to proclaim his conviction that God's Word was supreme in the universe. At issue and always before him was the necessity to proclaim His Word (see Isaiah 40).

 BEHIND THE SCENES

Isaiah has been called the "messianic prophet" and the "evangelistic prophet." He prophesied of both the first and second advents of Christ. His message spoke not only to those of his day but to the peoples of all time.

His name means "salvation," which aptly describes his message. He often focused on holiness, directing his contemporaries to cease from their social injustice, their quest for carnal indulgence, their trust in the arm of the flesh, and their hypocritical pretense of orthodox religion.

God's Word to Isaiah reveals a great deal of His will for people of all generations to live in righteousness. At the same time, the prophet draws attention to the Messiah, pointing to the King of all Righteousness, who alone is able to deliver us from ungodliness. This is the "Good News!"

BEHIND THE SCENES

Prophets in the Old Testament were men who were inspired of God, often with messages concerning future events. Their inspiration was the result of direct communication from God, not from conclusions arrived from personal experiences and observations.

They spoke as the Holy Spirit moved upon them with divine wisdom, knowledge, and understanding. They were often ridiculed and rejected because they frequently preached of God's impending judgment upon those who lived in disobedience to God's laws.

There is considerable debate concerning the role of prophets in the New Testament. Some believe their office no longer exists, that it was done away with at the advent of Jesus. Others believe in a New Testament fivefold ministry which includes apostles, prophets, evangelists, pastors, and teachers. Holding to this belief, it must be understood that the presence of the body of Christ as a New Testament entity, deputized with Christ's power and authority, makes the current office of the prophet somewhat different than it was in the Old Testament. Today, a prophet's ministry still must be inspired of God, but is largely to be a message confirming God's direction rather than giving it. The Holy Spirit is presently here to give guidance. Believers should be extremely cautious when prophetic words seek to initiate personal direction.

Look up the following verses in Psalms 107 and 119 and note what the Word of God is and does.

Name the two things God sent His Word to do. (Ps. 107:20)

What are the two things God's Word is said to be? (Ps. 119:105)

How can a young person keep his life clean? (Ps. 119:9)

Where did the psalmist hide God's Word? (Ps. 119:11)

What can the Word of God do for us personally? (Ps. 119:107)

What is one of the main qualities of God's Word? (Ps. 119:140)

What part of our bodies are we to use to propagate God's Word? (Ps. 119:172)

PROBING THE DEPTHS

Nothing is ultimately more important in our preaching and teaching than telling people about Jesus. Notice some of the principal parts of the message.

- Jesus is the manifestation of God in bodily form. (John 1:1; Col. 1:15–17; 2:9)
- God so loved the world that He sent Jesus to save it. (John 3:16)
- Jesus is the only way to the Father. (Acts 4:12)
- Jesus' shed blood is the only cleansing for sin. (Eph. 1:7; Heb. 9:22)
- Jesus is currently seated at the right hand of the Father interceding for us. (Heb. 7:25; 10:12)
- Jesus sent the Holy Spirit to guide and comfort us. (John 15:26)
- Jesus is coming again. (John 14:3)

PLACEMENT FOR MINISTRY

Jesus has wisely given to His body certain specialized parts to help keep certain key areas of life functioning. In our bodies these would correspond to our organs (heart, lungs, kidneys, etc.). What are these specialized parts in the body of Christ? (Eph. 4:7–12.)

According to Eph. 4:12, what key function do they serve?

What two things result from the proper functioning of the key parts?

Apart from these specialized parts, how are the majority of other members of the body equipped to function? (v. 7; 1 Pet. 4:10; Rom. 12:3–8)

FAITH ALIVE

In some people's minds, the job of the minister (or church staff) is to win souls. However, some submit to the pastor's prodding and periodically agree to "help" him win and train souls. The biblical pattern is that the *minister is to equip the layman* and together they do the work of ministry.

How do various programs in your church (classes, worship services, sports, concerts, etc.) provide tools to aid the evangelistic ministry of the body?

How many ministers does your church have? 1, 2, . . . 3? Or 100 or 1,000? Every believer is a minister! Each is an able and vital part of the body of Christ, doing His will in this world.

How would you answer someone who asked you, "What's the name of your minister?"

How can we avoid comparing our gift(s) with someone else in the body?

Jesus' goal for His church is to build it up by His Spirit. He does this by giving certain enabling abilities to the different parts He engrafted into the body. Paul analyzed these abilities in 1 Corinthians 12:4–6.

What three kinds of differences did he point out?

Which "diversity" or "difference" would fit the following definition?
- a special capacity or function
- sphere of service
- degree of power

KINGDOM EXTRA

In 1 Corinthians 12:14–26, Paul illustrated the necessity for this variety from the analogy of the human body. He pointed out the mutual dependence of all members.
- We ought to realize that we need each other. The Christian life cannot be lived alone. The body ought not reject members who have been grafted in.
- We ought to respect each other, and not think less of someone with less spectacular gifts.
- We ought to sympathize with each other. The secular world took note of the early Christians and agreed: "Behold how they love one another!"

According to 1 Corinthians 12:7, what is the source of these spiritual gifts?

What is described as the overall purpose of these gifts? (12:8–11)

In practical terms, there is no comparison between the infant church and the structured institution we know today as far as simplicity and effectiveness are concerned. Yet the unfinished task of spreading the "good news" of God's grace for forgiveness and power for deliverance would be an impossibility for us, too, except for the supernatural gifts of the Holy Spirit.

KINGDOM EXTRA

Distinguishing among the gifts of Romans 12:6–8 (from the Father), the gifts of 1 Cor. 12:8–10 (from the Holy Spirit) and those here [Eph. 4:11], which are explicitly given by Christ the Son (v. 8), is pivotal in comprehending the whole scope of spiritual gifts.[1]

In the New Testament we can see examples of different kinds of spiritual gifts involved in different kinds of evangelism. But the predominant form of evangelism evident in the Book of Acts and many epistles was "body evangelism." This is where the body of Christ is moving under the direction of the Holy Spirit, and new life inevitably results.

In seeking to spread the "good news," our goal should be to discern and activate our common "gifts" in this body of Christ. As we do, we must reject the tendency to compare our gift with someone else's. They are not given to compete but to complement each other. If we compare gifts we'll inevitably become discouraged as we see our own limitations and liabilities. However, if we will seek to discover, affirm, and release the giftedness of others, we will be liberated to be ourselves. And the end result will be the body of Christ is strengthened and the task of evangelism advanced.

FAITH ALIVE

Let's seek to emulate the best qualities of the New Testament church. We must start reaffirming and yielding to the true life of the body of Christ:

- giving ourselves to the equipping power of the Holy Spirit
- giving ourselves to the proclamation of the Word of God
- giving ourselves to the encouragement and cultivation of ministries in all members of the body.

---

1. *Spirit-Filled Life Bible* (Nashville: Thomas Nelson Publishers, 1991), 1792, "Kingdom Dynamics: Eph. 4:11, The Gifts Christ Gives."

Lesson 12/*Evangelizing in the End Times*

Evangelism during the "end times" will be both exciting and challenging. The work of the Spirit of God will provide great opportunities, but the work of the spirit of the Antichrist (1 John 4:3) will produce great opposition.

Peter predicted that in the end times immoral and greedy false teachers will promote their own selfish goals through destructive doctrines and private interpretations.

> But there were also false prophets among the people, even as there will be false teachers among you, who will secretly bring in destructive heresies, even denying the Lord who bought them, and bring on themselves swift destruction. And many will follow their destructive ways, because of whom the way of truth will be blasphemed. By covetousness they will exploit you with deceptive words; for a long time their judgment has not been idle, and their destruction does not slumber (2 Pet. 2:1–3).

Key phrases in Peter's prophecy include "destructive heresies," "destructive ways," and "deceptive words." How could these things frustrate evangelism in the end times?

WORD WEALTH

Heresies, *hairesis* (*hahee*-res-is); *Strong's #139. Compare "heresy" and "heretical."* From *haireomai,* "to choose." The word originally denoted making a choice or having an option. Progressing to a preference because of an opinion or a sentiment, it easily slipped into a mode of disunity, choosing sides, having diversity of belief, creating dissension, and substituting self-willed opinions for submission to the truth. The dominant use in the New Testament is to signify sects, people professing opinions independent of the truth.[1]

In the face of these challenging end-time circumstances, effective evangelism will require personal and congregational discipline, discernment, and devotion. Our Lord's remarks to the "candlestick congregation" at Ephesus, in the Book of Revelation, give insight as to how we can apply these key qualities to our lives and churches today.

WHAT ARE CANDLESTICK CONGREGATIONS?

The King James Bible translates the Greek word *luchnos(nia)* as "candle" or "candlestick." All modern translations give the more literal "lamp" or "lampstand." The difference is significant: a candle will burn and consume itself; a lamp contains oil and a wick and can continue to burn and give light if its oil is replenished and its wick consistently trimmed.

What does this description of a lamp's function say about spiritual renewal and holy living in a local church?

In Revelation 2:1–7, Jesus said to the church at Ephesus that He "walks in the midst of the seven golden lampstands" (v. 1). This suggests an intimate concern and care for the local assemblies of believers. He is the One who fills (and refills) the oil, and trims (and even replaces) the wick, as needed.

What could this suggest about spiritual renewal and leadership in a local church?

Do you need more oil in your lamp? Do you need your wick trimmed? Have you burned out?

BEHIND THE SCENES

The "candlesticks" were actual churches in John's day, but they also seem to have been "parable churches" to give heavenly instruction throughout all generations of the church (2:7, 11, 17, 29; 3:6, 13, 22). Each letter included:

- an accusation or commendation
- a call or directive
- a threat or a promise

The church in Ephesus was one of the leading congregations in Asia Minor. It probably began as a result of Paul's brief ministry there on his second missionary journey (Acts 18:18–21). The church was firmly established during Paul's extended stay on his third journey (Acts 19:1, 2, 6, 8–12, 20). His epistle to the Ephesians is rich in truth and doctrine, as well as guidance for practical Christian living.

AT A GLANCE

THE SEVEN CHURCHES OF REVELATION[2]				
	Commendation	Criticism	Instruction	Promise
Ephesus (2:1–7)	Rejects evil, perseveres, has patience	Love for Christ no longer fervent	Do the works you did at first	The tree of life
Smyrna (2:8–11)	Gracefully bears suffering	None	Be faithful until death	The crown of life
Pergamos (2:12–17)	Keeps the faith of Christ	Tolerates immorality, idolatry, and heresies	Repent	Hidden manna and a stone with a new name
Thyatira (2:18–29)	Love, service, faith, patience is greater than at first	Tolerates cult of idolatry and immorality	Judgment coming; keep the faith	Rule over nations and receive morning star
Sardis (3:1–6)	Some have kept the faith	A dead church	Repent; strengthen what remains	Faithful honored and clothed in white
Philadelphia (3:7–13)	Perseveres in the faith	None	Keep the faith	A place in God's presence, a new name, and the New Jerusalem
Laodicea (3:14–22)	None	Indifferent	Be zealous and repent	Share Christ's throne

In Revelation 2:2, what four things did He say had not gone unnoticed?

John also observed that they had faithfully disciplined those who professed Christianity but who persisted in practicing sin.

 KINGDOM EXTRA

The various problems and issues that arise in personal relationships and Christian fellowship may call for various levels of correction and discipline in Scripture: personal differences, doctrinal error, overt sin, gross immorality, a failing elder, and more. The Bible gives insightful guidelines to follow in faithfully discharging the church's duty to lovingly correct and discipline in these cases. Often such action is the responsibility of the "shepherds" and "overseers" of the congregation, "for they watch out for your souls, as those who must give account" (Heb. 13:17).[3]

What principles concerning church discipline can you find in the following scriptures?

Matt. 18:17–18

2 Thess. 3:6–12

1 Tim. 5:17–21

1 Tim. 6:3–5

2 Tim. 2:24–26

Titus 3:9–11

Heb. 12:11

James 5:19–20

Jude 22-23

Additionally, the Ephesian church was commended because they not only practiced church discipline, but also *discernment* "You have tested those who say they are apostles and are not, and have found them to be liars" (Rev. 2:2). They wisely linked the integrity of the messenger with the authority of the message.

It is difficult for church leadership to "try the spirits" (1 John 4:1) of forceful, charismatic personalities. But they must. Shepherds must protect the sheep from every semblance of sin, sham, and "shtick." "But we have renounced the hidden things of shame, not walking in craftiness nor handling the word of God deceitfully, but by manifestation of the truth commending ourselves to every man's conscience in the sight of God" (2 Cor. 4:2).

What kind of things concern you about the lifestyles or ministry practices of certain preachers or teachers?

How have these things affected their testimonies, before believers or non-believers? (2 Cor. 5:11, 12)

How can you discern the difference between what is merely *ministry style* and what is *ministry substance?*

How did Paul describe the balanced ministry he sought to model? (1 Thess. 1:5)

The apostle John, in his earlier epistles, gave guidelines for passing judgment on prophet-types. These guidelines concerned their doctrines and their deeds. Study the following passages and state the guidelines.

Doctrine (1 John 4:1–3):

Deeds (1 John 5:1–5):

After commending the Ephesian saints for their tenacity to truth and the work, Jesus indicted them for losing their devotion to Him, "Nevertheless, I have this against you, that you have left your first love" (v. 4).

In Paul's epistle to the Ephesians, thirty years before, he commended them for their "love for all the saints" (Eph. 1:15–16). Early on, they were noted for their love. Possibly their efforts in church discipline had left them with a harsh and condemning attitude, and they lost their love, warmth, and compassion for fellow saints.

What do you sense in your congregation? Joyous abandonment to God? to God's people? to God's work in the world?

Or do you sense complaints, criticism, pettiness, jealousy, or strife?

What accusations and/or commendations might the Lord of the church give to *your* congregation?

RENEWING CANDLESTICK CONGREGATIONS

In Revelation 2:5, the Lord Jesus gave both the course for correction and a word of warning to all congregations: "Remember therefore from where you have fallen; repent and do the first works, or else I will come to you quickly and remove your lampstand from its place—unless you repent."

Again, the lampstand represented the local church. Unless the Ephesians repented and restored their corporate devotion (Rev. 2:5) for Jesus and each other, the living Lord would remove the usefulness of that local church. They would no longer be "candlestick-quality," unless they got back to that former position of love and devotion.

Can you identify churches whose former glory is gone, whose candlestick has apparently been removed?

What can be learned about the importance of love in a local church from the following scriptures?

1 Cor. 13:1–7

Eph. 4:31–32

Phil. 2:1–4

How would these timeless expressions of love impact world evangelism in the end times?

 KINGDOM EXTRA

In Matthew 24:14, Jesus linked the worldwide witness of the gospel to His Second Coming. The text contains: 1) an anticipation of ministry—"This gospel . . . will be preached," involving the declaration of the kingdom message of grace for forgiveness and power for deliverance; 2) an arena of effort—"to all the nations," including every group of people; 3) a certainty of "signs" for a witness (see Mark 16:15–20), insuring "proof" of Christ's resurrection life and present power to save and heal. How pointedly Jesus' words speak of the Father's desire toward the nations of the world: God cares for all people; Jesus died for every person; and the Word of God is for every nation—before "the end."[4]

Today, Ephesus is an archaeological ruin. The church and the city it sought to redeem have been removed. Verse seven says "he who has an ear, let him hear what the Spirit says to the churches." Churches that are active in *the work of the Lord* but deficient in their love for *the Lord of the work* should listen and learn. Repentance precedes renewal and results in the kind of holy living which will enable world evangelism in the end-times.

END-TIME EVANGELISM AND HOLY LIVING

There has perhaps never been a greater hindrance to evangelism than real or perceived sin in the lives of believers. People who do not "walk the talk" become excuses by which unbelievers feel justified to stay that way. Second Peter 3:10–12 shows a connection between end-time events and evangelism:

> But the day of the Lord will come as a thief in the night, in which the heavens will pass away with a great noise, and the elements will melt with fervent heat; both the earth and the works that are in it will be burned up. Therefore, since all these things will be dissolved, what manner of persons ought you to be in holy conduct and godliness, looking for and hastening the coming of the day of God, because of which the heavens will be dissolved, being on fire, and the elements will melt with fervent heat?

What relationship does holiness and godliness have with the coming Day of the Lord?

Conversely, what relationship would a disregard for holy living and holy purposes have with the coming of Christ?

In recent years the moral and ethical failures of some big-name preachers and religious personalities have embarrassed the cause of Christ. As a result, many believers withdrew from sharing their faith with others. They felt the need to regroup rather than reach out.

END-TIME EVANGELISM AND PRAYER

In Revelation 5:6–9, the apostle John saw a Lamb in heaven who had been slain. Then he heard the heavenly hosts singing a "new song" to the Lamb, saying: "You are worthy to take the scroll, and to open its seals; for You were slain, and have redeemed us to God by Your blood out of every tribe and tongue and people and nation" (5:9).

Sandwiched between what John saw and what he heard was this fascinating description of the ones singing the new song: "Now when He had taken the scroll, the four living creatures and the twenty-four elders fell down before the Lamb, each having a harp, and golden bowls full of incense, which are the prayers of the saints. . . . For you were slain and have redeemed us to God by Your blood out of every tribe and tongue and people and nation, and have made us kings, and priests to our God" (5:8–9).

Somehow salvation is connected to the prayers of the saints. If Jesus died to redeem all peoples, then all peoples must hear the Good News. We who are called to the roles of "a royal priesthood" must give ourselves to prayer and intercession for "the nations."

What did God promise to give His Son, as the interceding Messiah, in Psalm 2:8?

How did Christ's high priestly prayer (John 17) include intercession for all future believers? (v. 20.)

WORD WEALTH

Make intercession, *entunchano* (en-toong-*khan*-oh); *Strong's #1793.* To fall in with, meet with in order to converse. From this description of a casual encounter, the word progresses to the idea of pleading with a person on behalf of another, although at times the petition may be against another.[5]

How do we "come boldly to the throne of grace?" (Heb. 4:14–16)

Why should we make sure our hearts are clean before God before we seek to intercede for others? (Ps. 66:18; 139:23–24)

Fasting is a discipline for focusing our prayers and intercessions. It pushes away distractions and helps us concentrate upon the Father.

How long did Jesus fast? (Matt. 4:2)

How were the evangelistic efforts of the early church enhanced by the practice of fasting? (Acts 13:1–3)

How did fasting enter in to the practice of leadership selection and ordination in the early church? (Acts 14:21–23)

KINGDOM EXTRA

Leaders of the early church arrived at decisions only after fasting and prayer. In Antioch the prophets and teachers fasted and prayed, seeking God's direction for the church. While they waited on God, the Holy Spirit gave direction (v. 2), thus beginning the missionary ministry, which eventually took the gospel to the whole world. Godly leaders rely on God for the direction and the empowering of their lives and ministry. Disciplined fasting and constant prayer are proven means for this, and as such, are mandatory in the lives of leaders (Matt. 9:15).[6]

How did Paul tie prayer and evangelism together? (1 Tim. 2:1–4)

Why should we pray for a quiet and peaceful climate? (1 Tim. 2:3–4)

How are prayers for our civic leaders related to an evangelistic harvest?

END-TIMES EVANGELISM AND WORSHIP

In his first pastoral letter, Peter wrote that those who come to Christ need to focus on two priorities, worship and witness. "Coming to Him as to a living stone, rejected indeed by men, but chosen by God and precious, you also, as living stones, are being built up a spiritual house, a holy priesthood, to offer up spiritual sacrifices acceptable to God through Jesus Christ. . . . But you are a chosen generation, a royal priesthood, a holy nation. His own special people, that you may proclaim the praises of Him who called you out of darkness into His marvelous light" (1 Pet. 2:4, 5, 9).

In verse 5 believers are described as what three things?

What is said to be the purpose of being "a holy priesthood"?

Rather than the sacrifices of bulls and goats, as were offered by the Old Testament priests, what kind of sacrifices are to be offered by New Testament priests? (Heb. 13:10–15)

Why is praising God a sacrifice?

PROBING THE DEPTHS

In the opening of Revelation, John introduces himself as a brother and companion in the struggle we all face (v. 9). His words "in the kingdom and patience of Jesus Christ" point to the dual facts of Christ's present kingdom triumph and the ongoing presence of evil and warfare that exact the patience of the church in the kingdom advances among and through us. In prefacing the broad arenas of prophecy about to be unfolded, John addresses two very important present truths: 1) We, Christ's redeemed, are loved and are washed from our sins—a present state (v. 6). 2) We, through His glorious dominion, have been designated "kings and priests" to God—also a present calling. Thus, these dual offices give perspective on our authority and duty and how we most effectively may advance the kingdom of God.

First, we are said to be kings in the sense that under the King of kings we are the new breed—the reborn, to whom God has delegated authority to extend and administrate the powers of His rule. Of course, this involves faithful witness to the gospel in the power of the Spirit and loving service to humanity in the love of God. But it also involves confrontation with dark powers of hell, assertive prayer warfare, and an expectation of the miraculous works of God (2 Cor. 10:3–5; Eph. 6:10–20; 1 Cor. 2:4). However, this authority is only fully accomplished in the spirit of praiseful worship, as we exercise the office of "priests." Some translations read, "a kingdom of priests," which emphasizes that the rule is only effective when the priestly mission is faithfully attended. Worship is foundational to kingdom advance. The power of the believer before God's throne, worshipping the Lamb, and exalting in the Holy Spirit of praise, is mightily confounding to the Adversary. (See Ex. 19:5–7, Ps. 22:3; Ps. 93:2; 1 Pet. 2:9)[7]

What are other forms of sacrifices with which God is pleased? (Rom. 12:1–2; Heb. 13:16)

Many people are won to Christ through the example of the sacrificial service and the praise of God's people. Deliverance, healing, and spiritual refreshing can be released when God's people praise and worship Him.

David declared that praise will bring the presence of God into our situations: "You are holy, enthroned in the praises of Israel" (Ps. 22:3). End-time worshipers should expect evangelism to take place in the environment of genuine praise. Exalt Jesus and expect a harvest!

 KINGDOM EXTRA

Jack Hayford, author of many choruses and worship songs, including the modern classic "Majesty," has said: "Few principles are more essential to our understanding than this one: the presence of God's kingdom power is directly related to the practice of God's praise. The verb 'enthroned' indicates that whenever God's people exalt His name, He is ready to manifest His kingdom's power in the way most appropriate to the situation, as His rule is invited to invade our setting.

"It is this fact that properly leads many to conclude that in a very real way, praise prepares a *specific* and *present* place for God among His people. Some have chosen the term 'establish His throne' to describe this 'enthroning' of God in our midst by our worshiping and praising welcome. God awaits the prayerful and praise-filled worship of His people as an entry point for His kingdom to 'come'—to enter, that *His* 'will be done' in human circumstances (see Luke 11:2–4; Ps. 93:2). We do not manipulate God, but align ourselves with the great kingdom truth: *His* is the power, ours is the privilege (and responsibility) to welcome Him into our world—our private, present world or the circumstances of our society."[8]

END-TIME EVANGELISM AND SPIRITUAL WARFARE

An important lesson on evangelism and spiritual warfare is taught in the Mark 9 account of Jesus' healing a boy who suffered from seizures. The symptoms indicated the sickness was serious, but the basic problem was an evil spirit which controlled his body.

How long had the boy had the physical symptoms mentioned in Mark 9:17–20?

How do we know this boy was harassed by an evil spirit? (See vv. 17, 18, 20, 25, 29.)

It seems that is not uncommon for manifestations of demonic influence in human bodies to overlap the symptoms of certain mental, emotional, or physical disorders. Whatever the symptom, Jesus looked past it to the source and brought deliverance and healing.

 KINGDOM EXTRA

In Mark 9:29 Jesus explained why the disciples' prayers had been fruitless in seeing the boy healed: "This kind can come out by nothing but prayer and fasting."

His explanation teaches: 1) some (not all) affliction is demonically imposed; and 2) some kinds of demonic bondage do not respond to exorcism, but only to fervent prayer. Continuance in prayer, accompanied by praise and sometimes fasting, provides a climate for faith that brings deliverance.[9]

 PROBING THE DEPTHS

Many lessons can be learned about deliverance from the devil and his demons by focusing on the ministry of Jesus in the Gospel of Mark.

- Expelling demons was a normal part of Jesus' ministry. (Mark 1:32–34, 39)
- Jesus cast out demons with authority! (Mark 1:21–27)
- Jesus spoke to demons as personalities, not abstract forces of superstitions. (Mark 5:6–13)
- Often exorcism was accomplished with unpleasant physical manifestations. (Mark 9:20, 25–26)
- Jesus gave his disciples authority to demonstrate the devil's defeat by casting out demons in His Name. (Mark 6:7, 12–13; 16:15–18)

End-time evangelism will be enhanced as we teach and train believers about spiritual warfare. They must learn practical steps of discipleship and deliverance from the Evil One (Matt. 6:13). Many have been strengthened by following these three steps:

1) *Confess* Jesus as your personal Lord and Savior; 2) *Cancel* any demonic curse, control, or contact by repenting of any occult or spiritualistic practices or paraphernalia; and 3) *Command* Satan and his demons to depart forever from your life, family, home, and possessions.

END-TIME EVANGELISM AND THE KINGDOM

Evangelism in the end times will increasingly be done by those who learn to partner in spiritual warfare with Christ's ongoing victory on the Cross. Those who would receive and spread the good news of life, health, and deliverance that Jesus did (Luke 4:18) will be those who come to perceive His purpose for them and participate in the present work of His Kingdom. This "kingdom mentality" is not superficial nor argumentative. It is powerful and authoritative. It is dynamic without being "pushy."

Evangelism will be effective when believers perceive the truth of God's kingdom and function daily under the authority of the King who is "not willing than any should perish but that all should come to repentance" (2 Pet. 3:9).

How is the timing of the Lord's return related to the condition and activity of the church? (2 Pet. 3:12; Matt. 24:14; Acts 3:19–21.)

PROBING THE DEPTHS

John's prophecy in Revelation 12 [relates to]: 1) the ongoing warfare on Earth (v. 9); 2) the overcoming ability of the redeemed because "the kingdom" has come (v. 10); 3) the two-edged truth that their victories often cost martyrdom (v. 11); and 4) the basis of their triumph: the Cross ("the blood of the Lamb") and the authority of God's Word ("the word of their testimony"— v. 12).

Various interpretive systems see this at different times within redemptive history. The mixture of pre-, a-, and postmillennial viewpoints has often fragmented the church, rather than providing a common base of wisdom for each group to receive while embracing one another as, presently, we all face a common Adversary (v. 9). Seeing that no complete interpretive scheme will be verified until after Christ comes, our wisdom is to embrace the Cross as our salvation and our source of overcoming victory. Then we can enter the conflict in confidence, knowing we shall triumph even though circumstances temporarily set us back. In the time of conflict, it will make no difference who was "right," but only that we were on the Messiah's side in this agelong spiritual struggle.[10]

We must be careful not to develop a mean-spirited intolerance toward those who are not of the household of faith. This unloving approach to the nonbelieving community gives credence to the Antichrist spirit that is present in our end-times culture. It creates a backlash that sweeps away the potential for evangelism and spiritual reconciliation.

CONCLUSION

Rather than surrender to the "spirit of this age," Pastor Jack Hayford has suggested that the church rise in faith and obedience as Abraham's seed (Gen 12:3; Rom. 4:16–17) to determine the destiny of nations. He says:

"It is neither pretentious nor arrogant to propose both: (1) the future of America is seriously imperiled, but salvageable; (2) the people whose faith and action are rooted in God's call and promise are the sole instruments who can introduce this salvation. There are ten steps I see—ours to take in faith and obedience, or to neglect . . . in surrender to futility.

1. *Believe the Promise*—(2 Chron. 7:14 and 15)

The beginning point is to decide that the power of prayer is potentially effective to bring a saving turnaround, and that such prayer is underwritten by the Almighty Himself.

2. *Love the Body* (Rom. 12:3)

Mutual respect and acceptance among all God's redeemed is essential. But this requires an end to suspicion, criticism, judgmentalism, and separatism.

3. *Bless Your Enemies* (Matt. 5:44)

The stance toward those opposed to our best interest as a people must be changed from one of snobbish and condescending anger to a posture of releasing, intercessory blessing.

4. *Pursue Peace* (Ps. 34:14; 1 Pet. 3:11)

The embracing of every ethnic group is required by the mandate of the Creator, who "has made from one blood every nation of men." Transethnic reconciliation is God's order.

5. *Live in Purity* (Phil. 2:14–15)

The Word of God, lived out by the early church, showed that the way to assert moral superiority in a corrupt culture is to shine by example, not shoot as an adversary.

6. *Value Life* (Prov. 31:8)

The issues of abortion and euthanasia are not political ones, but morally decisive ones. Our commitment to life is born of a respect for the Creator's world.

7. *Invade Violence* (Matt. 11:12)

The living church is not an institution, but an incarnation of Jesus Christ—His body, called to enter Hell's terrain, not run from its intrusions, reaching with life and love.

8. *Serve the Needy* (Matt. 5:16)

The ministry of the gospel involves compassion for the social need of humankind, as well as man's spiritual need. Good works create a platform for truth to be listened to.

9. *Preserve Liberty* (Rom. 13:1–7; 1 Tim. 2:1–4)

Responsible exercise of our privilege as free citizens and faithful attention to our responsibilities as believing intercessors are tools to employ.

10. *Demonstrate, Declare, and Dispense the Gospel* (Rom. 5:20)

As living evidences of the resurrected Savior (demonstrating Him), let us be giving people—who present the truth with winsomeness and power, as the Holy Spirit fills us for the task."[11]

1. *Spirit-Filled Life Bible* (Nashville: Thomas Nelson Publishers, 1991), 1920–1921, "Word Wealth: 2 Pet. 2:1 heresies."

2. *Nelson's Complete Book of Bible Maps and Charts* (Nashville: Thomas Nelson Publishers, 1993), 487.

3. Jack W. Hayford, *Pathways to Pure Power* (Nashville: Thomas Nelson Publishers, 1994), 36–37.

4. *Spirit-Filled Life Bible,* 1452, "Kingdom Dynamics: Matt. 24:14, The Gospel and 'The End.'"

5. Ibid., 1880, "Word Wealth: Heb. 7:25 make intercession."

6. Ibid., 1650, "Kingdom Dynamics: Acts 13:1–3, Fasting and Prayer."

7. Ibid., 1960, "Kingdom Dynamics: Rev. 1:5, 6, Worship and Praise."

8. Ibid., 770–771, "Kingdom Dynamics: Ps. 22:3, 'Establishing' God's Throne."

9. Ibid., 1486, "Kingdom Dynamics: Mark 9:22, 23, Cultivating a Climate of Faith for Healing."

10. Ibid., 1977–1978, "Kingdom Dynamics: Rev. 12:10, 11, NT: Agelong Warfare."

11. Jack W. Hayford, *Ten Steps Toward Saving America* (Van Nuys, Calif.: Living Way Ministries, 1994).